I. Ira Goldenberg

Oppression and Social Intervention

essays on the human condition and the problems of change

Nelson-Hall/Chicago

Library of Congress Cataloging in Publication Data

Goldenberg, I   Ira, 1936–
   Oppression and social intervention.

   Bibliography: p.
   Includes index.
   1. Social institutions—United States.   2. Power
(Social sciences)   3. Social action.   4. Oppression
(Psychology)   5. Political participation—United States.
I. Title.
HN65.G58   301.5'0973   78–6869
ISBN 0–88229–349–4 (cloth)
ISBN 0–88229–601–9 (paper)

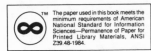

DEDICATION

To my parents
Fannie and Nathan Goldenberg
You fought the good fight
Now you are tired
Thank you for everything

And to our children
Ari, Sair, Rachel, and Asa
For you the struggle is just beginning
May you meet it with courage and dignity

Contents

Preface

The human drama continually unfolds, almost as if guided by the momentum of its own incompleteness. Its possibilities assume their meaning through struggle. Both the noblest and meanest moments of our collective history as a species have emerged through the struggles to alter the conditions of bondage. Indeed, the whole of humankind is the unfinished story of oppression and the attempts to undo its obscenities to the human spirit.

The overall theme of this book is the reconstruction of society. The theme carries with it the belief, not only that the dehumanizing aspects of a social order can be changed, but also that the very process of changing the social order can be as ennobling of the human spirit as it is cleansing of the human condition.

The need for a radical reconstruction of American society is no longer a matter worthy of serious or extended debate. It will not be accomplished through a reenactment of predictably timid and overly self-conscious thrusts at the consequences, rather than the causes, of suffering. And it will certainly not be satisfied by equating social change with the momentary relief that may accompany the exorcism of Richard M. Nixon from the body politic. What is required, at least as a beginning, is a thoroughgoing analysis of the contradictions and possibilities of a superindustrialized technocracy whose very power and existence depends on the perpetuation of the powerlessness and expendability of those whose labors built it. The historically oppressive character of the

"American experience" is its own demon. It is not just our leaders that require the exorcist's touch, but also our institutions and ourselves.

In some ways this may be the worst time to be writing a book about oppression and social intervention. We have been witness to revelations and have felt revulsion for the crypto-fascist clique in the White House which attempted to further subvert the quality of our national life. We have seen passivity, resignation, and even fear take hold of the American people. But, even more than this, we seem to be caught at a particular moment when poor people, nonwhites, and women—the groups most historically and repeatedly excluded from the body politic—are more separated from each other and more fragmented than ever before. At a time when our country might once again be moved, however grudgingly and hesitantly, toward a reexamination of its collective consciousness, those whose unity is so crucial to that struggle appear to be newly estranged from each others' pain. It is a situation as sad as it is understandable.

The purpose of this book is to share with the reader a particular orientation toward the problems of oppression and social intervention, especially as those problems relate to the reconstruction of our society. It is written from the perspective of what has been called "community psychology" and is therefore limited by the professional, academic, and historical roots of that discipline. It is further limited (perhaps biased would be a better word) by being written by a particular community psychologist, one whose views and analyses have been molded by his experiences. But one does not apologize for one's experiences; one only states them and then traces the process (and logic) of their conversion into a theoretical perspective.

The book is organized so that it conveys the manner in which ideas and experiences continually interact to produce an analysis. In Chapter 1 (Toward a Definition of Oppression and Social Intervention) the phenomenological method is used as a means of understanding the conditions which both comprise the oppressive experience and separate the process of social intervention from other approaches to "change" which often masquerade in its guise.

The second chapter, on the other hand, is far more personal in nature. Starting from the assumption that social interventionists are made and not born, in this chapter the process is traced by which the social interventionist arrives at his or her position. In addition, the author describes the experiential ground out of which social action emerges as a personally relevant and legitimate mode of relating to the social order. Chapter 3 (Understanding the American Experience) constitutes the book's most theoretical chapter. In this chapter the American experience is defined and explicated in terms of its underlying assumptions concerning the human condition and the translation of those assumptions into a particular form of social order. What emerges is an interactional analysis in which certain values, myths, and institutional processes coalesce to produce an "oppression-inspiring" social matrix in which a basically indefensible exclusionary premise is translated into a cultural imperative. Finally, the exclusionary process is traced and its impact both on the poor and the affluent is described.

In Chapter 4 the actual problems, prospects, and practices of social intervention are considered. While this chapter is more concrete and practical than the one preceding it, its basic purpose is to illustrate the consequences of a particular conception of contemporary American society on the problems of social change. In Chapter 5, The New Conservatives, the author describes what he believes to be the underlying social disengagement of the 1970s and traces its origins through collective memories and experiences of the preceding decades. In addition, in the chapter the issue of the loss of control, around which alternative life-styles develop, is isolated.

In the book's final chapter, Toward a Conception of Human Possibilities, are defined those "universal needs" (e.g., the needs for a sense of self, personal impact, and transcendence) whose fulfillment, the author believes, must become the basis for a truly reconstructed society. What is presented is neither a theory of personality nor a view of personality development, but a set of constructs which both define the human condition and distinguish it from all other forms of being. This last chapter ends with a brief and admittedly painful discussion of the relationship of the university to the problems of oppression and social intervention.

All books have multiple authorship. This book is no different. Family, friends, and co-workers all contributed, if only by withdrawing while remaining available. I thank them all. Special gratitude and recognition go to Ben Hersey whose ideas and thoughts were instrumental in providing the basic structure and underlying logic for Chapter 3.

And, yes, Ari, Sair, Rachel, and Asa, Daddy's finally coming out to play.

1

Toward a Definition of Oppression and Social Intervention

Definitions are always mischievous creatures. They invariably restrict; they cannot liberate. Their function is to narrow discourse and set limits to fantasy. Nevertheless, they are useful devils for they keep us from leaping the walls of our own imagination. More importantly, they force us to be specific, even when, as is the case with such phenomena as "oppression" and "social intervention," the dangers of specificity—particularly premature specificity—are numerous. And so, we must always contend with definitions, ever mindful of the fact that our victories and defeats reveal themselves solely in terms of the degree to which we allow ourselves to be self-indulgent.

The purpose of this chapter is *not* to establish a common frame of reference. Given the subject matter of this book, the imprecision of the issues to be dealt with, and the obvious

1

emotionally overloaded quality of the enterprise as a whole, any attempt to develop a common frame of reference would be an exercise in futility. Rather, the purpose of this chapter is to share with the reader a *very particular orientation* toward the meaning of such terms as "oppression" and "social intervention." The rationale for proceeding in this manner is a simple one: in the absence of a genuine commonality (or, perhaps more realistically, when consensus is either elusive or improbable), it is best that a particular position be defined as unambiguously as possible. If unity is indeed unattainable, let discussion and argument follow along lines unencumbered by a misleading or disingenuous sense of connection.

On Oppression

Unless one approaches the problem of defining oppression with the supreme confidence of the empirical purist, one cannot avoid being immediately struck by the almost monstrous nature of the undertaking. Soon even the most rigid logical positivist finds himself floundering and groping, unable to isolate individual variables, finding it impossible either to reduce, or to extrapolate from some hypothetical construct, and, thus, finally running the entire definitional gamut.

How, then, does one proceed? How does one try to capture the essence of a "condition" that appears at once both incredibly simple and defiantly complex? More importantly, how does one depict a "fact of life" which embraces everyone but systematically strangles only some? For better or worse, we have chosen to approach the problem phenomenologically —to start by attempting to describe the experience itself.

Oppression is, above everything else, a condition of being, a particular stance one is forced to assume with respect to oneself, the world, and the exigencies of change. It is a pattern of hopelessness and helplessness, in which one sees oneself as static, limited, and expendable. People only become opressed when they have been forced (either subtly or with obvious malice) to finally succumb to the insidious process that continually undermines hope and subverts the desire to "become." The process, which often is both self-perpetuating and self-reinforcing, leaves in its wake the kinds of human beings who have learned to view themselves and their world as chronically, almost genetically, estranged. The end product is an individual who is, in fact, alienated, isolated, and insulated from the society of which he nominally remains a member. He and his society are spatially joined but psychologically separate: they inhabit parallel but nonreciprocal worlds. *Oppression, in short, is a condition of being in which one's past and future meet in the present—and go no further.*

To be oppressed is to be rendered obsolete almost from the moment of birth, so that one's experience of oneself is always contingent on an awareness of just how poorly one approximates the images that currently dominate a society. Thus, whether we are talking about the black person who can never seem to get a decent job or the middle-class white whose employment is always endangered (and embarrassed) by the whims of an exploding technology or an economy seemingly forever based on war and junk, we are necessarily dealing with *the experience of marginality.* There is, indeed, at least some existential continuity between the numbing life in Appalachia and the empty one in Middle America. The extreme differences in content are clear; but so, too, are the underlying similarities. In both instances we find symptoms which are almost classic in nature: withdrawal (into drugs or some other form of chemical dissociation), violence (toward those either similarly oppressed or randomly selected as symbolic of the oppressors), and despair (the deep, unabating sense of the meaninglessness and arbitrariness of life).

The experience of continual marginality and premature obsolescence brings with it an enduring sense of futility, an all-encompassing belief that victories have no form and defeats have no substance. Put somewhat differently, to be oppressed is to be denied the chance to fail honestly, especially in those areas of human concern which we have been taught to view with more than a little awe, if not outright reverence. The oppressed person cannot exploit his own creativity in the sense of experiencing the fullness of power which attends the maximum use of one's capacities. Those capacities remain essentially unknown, and the creativity is forever unknowable. Instead, the oppressed individual (or group) is exploited in the sense of continually being taken advantage of or made use of meanly or unjustly for someone else's profit. In the absence of possibilities to contend with, there are only probabilities. *The oppressed person is always dealing with the probable. He cannot succeed or fail—he can only survive. And mere survival, however glorified or imbued with spiritual meaning, is the essence of futility, the mark of an unlived life.*

So much for the oppressive experience. What of the conditions that both comprise and spawn that experience? Here too we must be more specific, for such terms as "racism," "sexism," "classism," and "generationalism," however seductive because of their apparent all-inclusiveness, fail to define the essential structures which inhibit individual and collective growth. What we are after are not the myriad causes, manifestations, and consequences of one or another form of human oppression. That we shall deal with later. What we seek to describe are the particular structures through which *all* forms of oppression express themselves and can be labeled.

The first of these structures may be called *containment*. All forms of oppression seek first and foremost to contain or limit the range of free movement available to a particular group. The containment may be physical or psychological (oftentimes it is both), but its primary function is to increasingly restrict and narrow the scope of possibilites that can be entertained. Fantasy is left alone; its purpose is to subvert reality. Thus, for example, whether one is referring to the obvious containment symbolized by the company town or the not so obvious containment that manifests itself through the practice of a studied and sophisticated tokenism, one is dealing with the quarantining of people from the possibilities of change. The mechanism may vary, but the objectives remain the same: to both isolate and control the development of people.

Let us look, for example, at the ways in which we deal with the young in our society, particularly adolescents and those youth whose behavior we eventually label as delinquent. Traditional approaches to the "problems" presented by adolescents have always been directed toward containing the adolescent in the hope and belief that controlling and/or otherwise limiting his or her behavior will facilitate the process by which existing social institutions can effectively remedy whatever problems are presumed to be endemic in that portion of the population. Implicit in the traditional (and treasured) conception of the problems confronting adolescents are the following assumptions upon which most adult-youth relationships are based: first, that adolescence (presumably unlike either childhood or adulthood) is a particularly stressful period that is both universal in nature and predictable in onset: second, that delinquent, nonconforming, or deviant acts by adolescents are both the result and concrete symptoms of inadequate, incomplete, or pathological socialization; and third, that existing societal values (particularly as reflected in the practices and orientations of the institutions charged with their protection, promulgation, and perpetuation) are not only sound, but also supportive of individual and collective self-determination and self-actualization.

The singular importance, of course, of the assumptions described above is that they provide what appears to be a consensually validated theory concerning the period of adolescence as a whole, and delinquent or deviant acts in particular. Even more interesting, however, is that the assumptions themselves provide a context and framework—a rationale—for adult-initiated and -controlled interventions designed to perpetuate the segregation of a major part of the population, while at the same time urging these youths to lend themselves to the ministrations of their keepers until they are deemed ready for social, political, and economic inclusion. Finally, the assumptions make clear the belief that the adolescent and his society stand in unalterable opposition to each other, and that the adversary nature of the relationship can only be changed if and when the adolescent capitulates. The act of capitulation is variously labeled as "adjustment" or increasing "maturity" and is taken as evidence that he has both identified with the perspectives of the adult world, and adopted them.

The problem, of course, is that there is very little evidence to either justify or support the theory, however parsimonious (not to mention comprehensive) that theory might appear. To begin with, the assumption concerning the uniqueness, universality, and predictability of adolescence as a period of intense stress is certainly open to question. Cross-cultural and anthropological data gathered over the past thirty years have clearly indicated the "culture-bound" nature of the phenomenon (Benedict, 1949; Hess & Goldblatt, 1957; Friedenberg, 1963). In essence, the data indicate that adolescence becomes a problem only in those cultures which, because of particular economic, social, and/or sexual legacies, actively exclude the adolescent from full societal participation. Thus, when Friedenberg refers to American adolescents as "among the last social groups in the world to be given the full nineteenth-century colonial treatment," he is describing a situation not borne of any social crises inherent in the development cycles surrounding puberty. Instead it is society, seeking to retain its traditional adult dominance and maintain economic and political stability, that first develops and then acts to confirm a host of treasured myths concerning its heirs—its youth.

The second assumption, that of the implicitly pathological character of most, if not all, delinquent acts, is similarly difficult to defend. If one accepts, even partially, a "colonialist interpretation" of the relationship between our society and its heirs, one is then also forced to redefine "deviance" and "deviant acts" within a context which now focuses attention on the behavioral consequences of one or another form of systematic isolation. For the adolescent, on a social level, isolation takes the form of legal exclusion and physical containment. On the psychological level, it manifests itself in a variety of institutionally induced crises revolving around such issues as personal worth, identity, competence, and responsibility. Finally, there currently do not exist any viable mechanisms for youth-initiated institutional change on the one hand, or even the simple redress of individual grievances on the other. It is, in short, a situation in which the "ruled" have little or no opportunities or options available to them through which they can in any significant and lawful way alter the conditions of their own captivity. Thus, whether we are talking about the delinquent act committed either by the alienated middle-class suburban teenager or the disenfranchised poor youth of the inner city, we are referring, almost by definition, to acts which, if not directly political in nature, are certainly "adaptive" with respect to the conditions that spawned them.[1] This adaptive (rather than pathological) interpretation of many acts previously considered deviant or delinquent is both explored and documented in the recent work of Brown (1965), Clark (1965), Gordon (1967), Liebow (1967), the Kerner Commission (1968), and Levine and Levine (1968).

The final assumption that existing institutions, especially those charged with the responsibility of socializing the young, both represent and practice values consistent with an ideology predicated on concepts of self-determination and self-actualization is, unfortunately, perhaps the easiest to refute. Simply put, the assumption is untrue. The current nature of our society, divided and fractured by what often seem to be irreparable racial, sexual, and class antagonisms, is the clearest and most damning evidence available. More concretely, however, the assumption itself rests on two premises. The first is that there exists some discernible and positive correlation between the rhetoric and day-to-day reality of our socializing institutions. Thus, for example, one would expect schools to focus their attention on the liberation of individuals and groups through the development of educational philosophies and processes stressing such fundamental values as trust, freedom, self-direction, and the intrinsic reward and excitement of the educational experience. Instead, as has been amply documented by the work of Goodman (1960), Kozol (1970), and Sarason (1971), both the learning experience and the social settings in which most formal learning currently takes place are, by and large, characterized by fear, the denial of individuality, and the affirmation of conformity, control, and coercion as appropriate mechanisms for shaping what is considered responsible behavior.[2] The second premise has to do with what might be called the quality of life within these institutions, particularly those directly charged with the task of socializing others. Here, too, the situation is more than a little sad, for we now have data that clearly indicate just how poor and empty the quality of life really is for those who work in these settings. For example, research by Sarason et al. (1966), McIntyre (1969), Slater (1970), and Goldenberg (1971) has raised some fundamental questions about the ability of settings which are themselves both "deviant" (i.e., racist, sexist, elitist, etc.) and "internally unhealthy" (i.e., closed off to processes of self-reflection) to foster health and productivity in others. It is, in short, a situation which suggests that our society's principal socializing institutions neither represent nor practice the values which they profess to hold and protect.

The point, of course, is that however illegitimate the theory, however questionable the assumptions, and however contradictory the premises, the end result is the development of programs and practices that serve to quarantine a large percentage of the population. The creation and perpetuation of social structures that *contain* the young, albeit by distorting their needs, is a social imperative: oppression cannot occur in the absence of such social imperatives.

A second structural characteristic is one we might call *expendability*. By expendability we mean social arrangements which create the kind of day-to-day reality through which individual and group distinctiveness ceases to have meaning in the interactions between human beings. Oppression cannot occur in the absence of structures which continually affirm the essential social expendability of certain people. Expendability takes many forms and assumes a variety of guises depending on the situation, but the unifying theme is one which stresses the "fact" that within a given group of people individuals can be replaced or substituted by others with no loss to the whole. Thus, whether one is speaking of the latest psychosurgical experimentation on inmates in our penal institutions (Mark & Ervin, 1970; Procumier, 1973; Chorover, 1973) or the administration of drugs to poor white and black elementary school children in inner-city public schools (DiMascio & Shader, 1970; Conners, 1971), one is dealing with situations which can only occur through the development of practices predicated on the assumption that specific groups, types, or classes of people are both expendable and replaceable.

In an even more general sense, one can view issues of social invention within the framework of the expendability concept. Mass production, the artificial creation of a mass ideology, and the manipulation of social symbols—all examples of the "medium" as McLuhan and Fiore (1967) define it—could not take place unless there already existed structures and contexts through which people had begun to experience and accept their own expendability. Clearly, at least for adults, these contexts occur mainly in what is called the "world of work" where the effortless substitution of machines for people and people for people merely accentuates what has come to be accepted as a dominant and inevitable fact of life. But even in areas usually thought to be governed by other kinds of norms, even more lasting norms, we begin to see evidence that structural expendability is becoming an integral part of the social or interactional process. One need only read carefully the work of Toffler (1970) or take seriously the implications of Lifton's (1968) concept of "protean man" to begin to appreciate the degree to which the notion of human expendability has intruded itself into both the ideologies that govern and the forms which embody human relationships.

The ultimate result, in behavioral terms, of structures which stress the fundamental expendability of people is the gradual but clear development of individual and group passivity. The more firmly entrenched the concept of expendability becomes, the more sophisticated are the social mechanisms through which that concept is mediated, and the more likely it is that people will begin to accept their own powerlessness to change the myths that govern their lives. One of the clearest expressions of the mounting and internalized sense of powerlessness is the growth of passivity—a curious passivity punctuated only by outbursts of violence, usually directed toward oneself or others similarly oppressed.[3] Indeed, it may very well be that much of the public hue and cry that greeted such books as Bobby Seale's *Seize the Time* and Rabbi Meir Kahane's *Never Again* had less to do with the specific programs they advocated than it did with the challenge to the prevailing views of Jews and blacks as dependent and/or reactive in their dealings with the reigning majority. Both the Black Panthers and the Jewish Defense League, their ultimate politics aside, began with a single purpose in mind: to destroy the notion that blacks and Jews were destined to remain either passive or expendable.

Somewhat related to the concept of expendability are those social structures which seek to *compartmentalize* people and, even more importantly, the ways in which they live. If, as we have tried to indicate, the oppressive experience is related to a chronic inability to feel a sense of personal dominion and completeness, then it stands to reason that there must exist certain structures which prevent this from occurring. It is in this sense that compartmentalization refers to the variety of ways in which people are prohibited from developing an integrated style of life; that is to say, a way of being that is not arbitrarily interfered with by the ever-narrowing roles, models, and images that define what is or is not acceptable in the many crucial settings that directly affect one's existence. In other words, compartmentalization is the process which encourages partial rewards at many levels but denies fulfillment at any one level. Thus, for example, we now "work in order to live": there is little or no relationship between ourselves and our work, between how we earn our living and what we do with that "life"; there is no continuity between our public and private worlds.

The compartmentalization of people, both within themselves and between themselves and others, creates the kinds of conditions through which the development and maintenance of a sense of community is incredibly difficult, if not totally impossible. Without a sense of community, without relationships between people, there ensues both isolation and weakness, the essential preconditions for one or another kind of exploitation.

We come, finally, to what may be the most important of the essential structures through which the oppressive experience is mediated: ideology. Ideology, obviously, is not a "thing." It is neither material nor does it assume any definitive or predictable form. It is, nevertheless, a structure, for it serves to shape and control our responses to events which impinge themselves upon our consciousness. Stated differently, without an appropriate ideology to fall back upon and to use as an overarching interpretive schema, such other structures as containment, expendability, and compartmentalization would not suffice to produce the oppressive experience. We do, of course, have such an ideological schema: *the doctrine of personal culpability.*

Stated in its simplest form, the doctrine of personal culpability is a socially conditioned psychological set. Its purpose is to both encourage and predispose individuals to interpret their shortcomings or failures, their essential incompleteness, as evidence of some basically uncontrollable and, perhaps, unchangeable personal deficit. The doctrine of personal culpability serves to detract and distract one from focusing attention on the systemic constraints to growth. It encourages the internalization of blame and the heaping of abuse upon oneself. It is, in short, the kind of doctrine through which those who have been purposefully contained, made to feel expendable, or otherwise manipulated are now encouraged to view their condition as not only inevitable, but also traceable to some mysterious personal deficiency. The result is the transformation of social injustice into a perverted form of poetic justice: the myth is maintained by making the victim believe himself to be the principal author of his own victimization.

Doctrines of personal and group culpability derive their power from a variety of sources, not the least of which is the parsimonious manner in which they appear to explain the past and justify the present. The theory of Social Darwinism, for example, is an eminently simple and seemingly tight rationale for a differential class structure. So too are the doctrines related to racial, generational, and sexual dominance. In each case, however, the fundamental purpose is the same: to impress upon those who have been excluded the legitimacy of the process of exclusion.

The ultimate test of the efficiency of the doctrine of personal culpability is the degree to which the exploited individual or group incorporates, adopts, or otherwise identifies with the message he is asked to accept about himself and his group. Such phenomena as Jewish self-hatred, or the often internalized rage which Grier and Cobbs (1968) describe as accompanyinig the purposeful inculcation of certain perceptions about and among blacks, are but the clearest examples of this process. Indeed, oppression would be incomplete were it not for the acceptance of the notion of personal culpability by those so entreated.

Social programs presumably designed to help the oppressed have often turned out to be among the most efficient mechanisms for perpetuating the doctrine of personal culpability. Let us look at a few recent examples. First, the so-called War on Poverty. The late-lamented War on Poverty was never really intended to be a war at all. At its very best it was a painfully timid and overly self-conscious assault on the consequences, rather than the causes, of human misery. It was the kind of program whose philanthropic appeal was from the very beginning basically devoid of the inevitable threat that would have accompanied it had its creators touted it as a crusade against the social, economic, and institutional foundations of our society. Consequently, the initial consensus that surrounded the War on Poverty was of the unthreatened and unembittered. They saw their lives, not as indictments of the American Dream, but rather as testaments to its validity. Unlike the target populations for whom it was intended, the War on Poverty was created by people whose faith in America and its institutions was as unshaken as their belief that poverty could be eliminated through the development of a massive program of individual remediation.

And that is the key: *individual remediation*. The War on Poverty was both an expression of and, more importantly, a vehicle for the perpetuation of the view that poverty was basically traceable to individual shortcomings on the part of poor people themselves.[4] Thus, whatever limited resources the War on Poverty had at its disposal were almost entirely devoted to "fixing up" individuals. Poverty was to be eradicated through more personalized forms of counseling, training, and education, through programs specifically aimed at "Pygmalionizing the poor," however varied and lofty the accompanying rhetoric. What was not stated was the obvious: that people were poor because they had no money, goods, or power in a society that judged worth specifically in those terms. What was not acted upon was equally obvious: that the barriers to possessing either goods or power were not created by the victimized but by the institutional sources of their victimization (Cloward, 1965). And so the War on Poverty, whatever its accomplishments, actually served to extend and reinforce the doctrine of personal culpability.[5]

A second example is the current programs of rehabilitation for drug addiction. Research recently completed on the practices of businessmen and drug treatment personnel with respect to their addict clients indicates the existence of what might almost be called a conspiracy aimed at keeping the so-called rehabilitated drug abusers unemployed (Goldenberg & Keating, 1973). In essence, the *Catch-22* scenario works as follows. Amid the pompous rhetoric of both businessmen and therapists concerning the need for concerted efforts to help the drug user become a "happier and more productive individual," clear reality emerges with stark simplicity: the reformed addict has no more of a chance of being involved in a treatment program that takes his employment needs seriously than Yossarian had in trying to make sense of the almost pathologically inverted values and behaviors of those who determined his fate. One finds, for example, that businessmen who possess the jobs, after affirming their unwavering commitment to the American ethos of self-improvement and "pulling oneself up by one's bootstraps," then promptly turn around and develop elaborate corporate mechanisms to prevent the people who have demonstrated some personal uplifting from becoming gainfully employed. On the other side, one finds the therapists and other professional helpers in drug rehabilitation programs first acknowledging the importance of "real life issues" in the rehabilitation of drug addicts and then blithely focusing their therapeutic interventions almost entirely on the hidden and often exotic libidinal forces presumed to be operating in their unemployed clients.

Let us forget, at least for the moment, the behavior of the businessmen described above. Historically, they have made little pretense about agonizing over the human condition or its broader social contexts. But what of the mental health professionals? How does one begin to understand their duplicity in this situation? The answer, I think, is once again to be found in the doctrine of personal culpability that underlies most of our existing theories of human dysfunctioning, particularly those which have served as the ideological girders upon which the helping professions have built their empires. There is a very "simple" reason for the therapist's inability or unwillingness to let the relatively "mundane" question of employment intrude itself in the rehabilitative process: it is the belief that somehow, in some vague, unspecified, and almost mystical manner, the truly healthy person will naturally and with little difficulty deal with the problem on his own. Mental health professionals, for all their exposure to the dark and brooding passions that supposedly lurk within the human spirit, remain incorrigible optimists. For them there is virtually nothing that the man or woman whose "head is together" cannot accomplish. A productive and well-paying job? No problem at all for the person who has learned to "cope." The demonstrated racism, sexism, and elitism of industry's hiring policies? A mere inconvenience to the person who has begun to resolve his inner conflicts. The dehumanizing blandness and emptiness of a job's contents? Little difficulty for the person who has his "thing together." In short, the heroic view that most mental health professionals have of man's infinite capacity to actualize himself once he is healthy makes it virtually unnecessary for the therapeutic process to address itself to the question of employment in any direct or central manner. The healthy man can fend for himself—or so say those whose relative comfort makes personal heroism unnecessary. People may succumb through no fault of their own to the ravages of systematically induced suffering, but the doctrine of personal culpability remains the basic ideological rationale for their pain.

There is little we can add to the foregoing attempt to define oppression. Using a phenomenological perspective as our starting point, we have tried to describe the experience as well as the social structures which both comprise and mediate that experience. Our analysis tends to view and define the problem of oppression in terms of the existence of certain social imperatives which manifest themselves through the promulgation of practices aimed at containing or otherwise limiting the development of people. These practices are invariably accompanied by doctrines which seek to create an air of respectability for the enterprise as a whole, the kind of respectability which serves not only to condone the oppressive process, but also to preserve and perpetuate it.

On Social Intervention

Unlike the situation with respect to the concept of oppression, the problem of defining social intervention requires that we pay almost as much attention to defining what it is not as we do to describing exactly what it is. At present, distinctly different and sometimes opposing viewpoints and social intentions have come to employ the same symbols and rhetoric. Both Richard Nixon and Huey Newton speak of "Power To The People," but they clearly mean different kinds of power for different groups of people. So, too, is it the case in the arena of social action. It is, for example, currently stylish for almost anyone, independent of how directly or indirectly he may be involved in the basic issues of change, to refer to himself as a "social change agent." Thus, we now find change agents tilling the soil on organic farming communes in Vermont, "Rolfing" each other at the Esalen Institute in California, or just plain trying to "make it through the night." They all proclaim that "my life is a political statement" and feel, quite honestly, a deep and unabating kinship with various movements for human liberation. Extreme examples aside, the problem is one of differentiating between those who claim to be social interventionists and those who actually are engaged in the work of social intervention. In order to make this distinction we must once again dispense with a false commitment to consensus and focus on the specific character and meaning of the concept of social intervention itself.

We might begin by taking a close look at the words "social" and "intervention." The term social implies two things: first, an approach which involves allies or confederates; and second, an orientation toward causality which goes beyond narrow explanations revolving around individual and/or interpersonal dynamics. To be engaged in things that are social is to work with others in cooperative and interdependent ways to effect change in institutions. Thus, the kind of individual manipulation symbolized by the actions of a mythical "President's analyst" would not be considered a social act. It would be an instance of personal leverage used to influence the behavior of a particularly powerful individual. The term social is reserved for actions that are both collective in nature and oriented toward broad institutional policies rather than the individuals temporarily empowered to carry out those policies.

The term intervention, on the other hand, always involves interference with an ongoing and often accepted social process. It is an intrusion of one sort or another, an attempt to change some existing pattern of functioning or set of social arrangements. The intention is to alter certain "regularities" and to either provide or extract alternative modes of "doing business." Thus, intervention always involves the introduction of "foreign elements" into a setting which was previously more or less homogeneous. The foreign elements can be new ideas or new actions, and they can be introduced by people either indigenous to or outside the setting, but their introduction is disruptive because they interfere and seek to affect the interests of those whose values have previously defined the setting's intentions.

Given the above, the concept of social intervention could be viewed as synonymous with the notion of institutional intrusion, for we are defining the issue in terms that stress three factors: collective action, an institutional focus, and an orientation toward altering existing practices and priorities. Clearly, the approach we have taken toward the problem of defining social intervention is replete with certain values. But, we would argue, there is no change that is value-free. Neither, as we shall indicate later, are there techniques which are value-free. Social intervention and social change are ultimately questions of values—values and strategies and the relationship between the two.

There are currently at least four different orientations toward the problems of social change. Each has at one time or another sought to depict itself as a form of social intervention. Whether or not any or all of these approaches are indeed examples of social intervention depends on the specific criteria one develops in order to define the social intervention model. We have already in a general way described our own interpretation of the term social intervention. Given that interpretation, we ought now to define more concretely some of the dimensions that become relevant in assessing the degree to which different orientations approach that definition. Having done that, we shall compare and contrast those orientations with the model of social intervention that emerges in order to analyze those dimensions.

DIMENSIONS OF SOCIAL INTERVENTION

1. *Degree of Identification with the Setting's Underlying Goals, Assumptions, and Intentions:* This refers to the essential congruity or fit between the fundamental values of the change agent and those of the setting or system in which he wishes or allows himself to become engaged. And by fundamental values we do not mean the rhetoric developed by the setting for public consumption (e.g., "the purpose of education is to liberate and prepare the individual to realize his or her own potential") or the jargon employed by the change agent (e.g., "to facilitate the development of openness, competence, and creativity"). Rather, we mean the basic political, social, and economic orientations of the two parties involved. *To the degree that there is a significant commonality or overlap between the values of the setting and those of the change agent, to that degree are we not dealing with an instance of social intervention.*

2. *Belief in the Need for Basic Systemic Change:* Related to the above is the question of the change agent's analysis of whether or not significant change is needed in the basic underlying structure of the setting with which he becomes involved. Here, too, we must distinguish between basic change (i.e., some fundamental shift in a setting's

orientations and/or priorities) and the minor reordering of existing practices and processes unaccompanied by any significant alterations in the allocation of institutional resources. *To the degree that relatively minor or symbolic changes are envisioned, to that degree are we not dealing with an instance of social intervention.*

3. *Source of Agency:*, This refers specifically to the question of whose agent the change agent really is. In other words, independent of how the change agent is brought into the setting or who brings him in, the issue is simply one of which group's interests are advanced by the change agent's behavior. All rhetoric aside, given the unequal distribution of power, resources, and control over intentions that characterize most social settings, the change agent cannot claim to be a disinterested party whose goals are simply to make certain skills or experiences available to the setting as a whole. In fact, he *has* a constituency, and he cannot be all things to all people. *To the degree that the change agent functions to legitimize, increase, make more palatable, mask, or otherwise perpetuate the orientations and objectives of those who control the setting, to that degree are we not dealing with an instance of social intervention.*

4. *The Problem of Process:* There are, unfortunately, a variety of ways in which the term "process" is both understood and used. For purposes of the distinctions currently being drawn, process refers to the manner in which people are exposed to the different ways in which they can either analyze or interpret the conditions under which they live. An "adaptive" orientation toward process would be one in which the change agent seeks to "turn people onto" the personal, interpersonal, and/or intragroup dynamics that define some of their problems. A "consciousness-raising" approach to process would be one in which the attempt is made to help people become more aware of the larger social forces that form the context in which their problems are embedded. *To the degree that the change agent approaches the problem of process from a basically adaptive perspective, to that degree are we not dealing with an instance of social intervention.*

Figure 1. Approaches to Change and the Dimensions of Social Intervention

CHANGE FOCUS	SPECIFIC APPROACH	Identity with setting Goals		Need for Basic Change		Source of Agency		Process Orientation		Peaceful Change	
		Yes	No	Yes	No	Setting	Others	Adaptive	Consciousness-Raising	Yes	No
Conservative → Radical											
I.	SOCIAL TECHNICIAN	X			X	X		X			X
II.	TRADITIONAL SOCIAL REFORMER	X			X		X	X		X	
III.	SOCIAL INTERVENTIONIST		X	X			X		X	X	
IV.	SOCIAL REVOLUTIONARY		X	X			X		X		X

In Figure 1 we summarized and illustrated the degree of fit between four different approaches to change and the dimensions of social intervention described above. Each approach has at one time or another labeled itself as a form of social intervention. The four approaches, listed in terms of the increasing "radicalism" of their overall orientation, are: the *social technician*, the *traditional social reformer*, the *social interventionist*, and the *social revolutionary*. In each case we shall offer a capsule description of how and in what ways the particular approach is either consistent or inconsistent with the model or dimensions of social intervention.

20

5. *Belief in the Changeability of the System Through Essentially Peaceful Means:* This, of course, refers to the change agent's fundamental assumption concerning the possibility of basic systemic change unaccompanied by wholesale violence or the total dismantling of existing institutional structures. The question has to do with the change agent's own analysis of whether or not the popular definition of revolution either makes sense or is a realistic possibility in a society which, in fact, does not have a revolutionary history or tradition. *To the degree that the change agent envisions violence and/or the total destruction of all existing institutional arrangements as the basic vehicle for systemic change, to that degree are we not dealing with an instance of social intervention.*

I. The Social Technician

In terms of the dimensions developed above, there is a significant difference between the social technician's orientation toward change and that of the social interventionist. The social technician actually functions as the guardian of the system. The results of his work generally show up as systems' maintenance rather than systems' change, regardless of the rhetoric that usually accompanies his style or techniques. The social technician appears in many forms, maintains that his orientation and skills are value-free, and often claims to be solely interested in increasing the sense of well-being and overall competence of the setting and those who inhabit it. In fact, the results of his efforts are to mute discontent, "cool" the situation, or otherwise inhibit the transfer of power and resources from those who control them to those who are controlled by them. The social technician identifies strongly with the institution's values, sees little need for any basic change, and encourages the adaptation of members to the system's needs through the application of a variety of techniques or tactics.

A few examples. Following the ghetto riots of the late-1960s, many mental health professionals undertook the training of nonprofessionals in the application of individual and group techniques for use in instances of "crisis intervention." Upon closer examiniation, especially by local community groups, such projects often were revealed to be rather elaborate attempts to employ inner-city people as defusers of community discontent in their own neighborhoods (CRRC, 1971). In the field of organizational behavior, much of Argyris' (1967) work, particularly at the State Department, could be viewed as consistent with a social technician's orientation. Rather than dealing explicitly with the relationship between foreign policy and internal process (the intervention took place at the height of the American military buildup and involvement in Vietnam), focus was directed at improving the pattern of communication among high-ranking State Department officials.[6] Finally, in the field of education, there are numerous examples of how the helping professions are employed by school systems to either isolate and remove troublesome students or to run workshops designed to help school personnel deal more effectively with school atmosphere, activities geared to focus attention away from the broader and more basic ideological, educational, and political issues which are at the root of much of the current unrest in our public educational institutions (Goldenberg, 1973).

The social technician is generally called into a situation when there is a problem as definied by those who control the setting. Such problems usually involve decreasing profits and efficiency, client or consumer unrest, or an increased questioning of the setting's values by those most directly affected by the setting's policies. The social technician's job is to check the problem as quickly as possible. Like his employers who control the setting, the social technician is fundamentally afraid of basic change, perhaps for two reasons: first, because his own interests would be endangered; and second, because at some deep level he views the masses as inherently violent and destructive in nature, as being incapable of handling the responsibility for determininig the direction of their own lives.

II. The Traditional Social Reformer

The traditional social reformer's approach to the problem of change is more like that of a broker than that of a social interventionist. He is a negotiator, an extractor of concessions, the eternal middleman endlessly seeking to traverse some imaginary bridge between those with power and those who are being destroyed by the use and misuse of that power. Although certainly modified by the passage of time, the traditional social reformer derives his strength from a continuing belief in the Lady Bountiful model of change: the poor and oppressed can be uplifted through the enlightened efforts of the more selfless among those who possess the resources to change conditions. His belief in the inherent perfectability of the system is as endless as his conviction that time, patience, education (both for the oppressed and their oppressors), and an unyielding appeal to rationality will inevitably result in good things happening. While rarely a member of a clearly exploited group, the traditional social reformer is a champion of the underdog who sees himself as working "for them," and, while he basically accepts the system as it exists, he acknowledges the need to somehow curb its excesses.

Two factors are important in understanding the model of change under which the traditional social reformer operates. The first is that his time perspective on change is incredibly long. Thus, he can continually urge the oppressed to be patient, accepting relatively small changes or concessions wrung from the system with the assumption that time and goodwill are the ultimate handmaidens of an improved lot. The second is that he perceives change as occurring most legitimately and effectively from the top down. Consequently, the empowerment of people themselves does not occupy a central place in his thinking. His mission is to extract concessions from the setting or system, and not to equip the oppressed to get the concessions for themselves. The traditional social reformer rarely shares his skills, analysis, or leverage with the people whose cause he champions. He retains his resources, guaranteeing the continued dependence of those he helps and the perpetuation of his own position of leadership.[7]

III. The Social Interventionist

Unlike the social technician and the traditional social reformer, the social interventionist is in basic disagreement with the underlying ideology and practices that guide the operation of most social institutions. In our society, this might take the form of opposition to such values as the presumed validity of the profit motive, the competitive ethos, class differences parading under the guise of a meritocracy, and the unequal allocation of opportunity, goods, and power (see Chapter 3). More concretely, however, the social interventionist is concerned with the consequences of that ideology on those whose lives are most directly and adversely affected by the social practices which emanate from such values. Thus, the social interventionist is always in a dilemma. On the one hand, he fundamentally disapproves of a conception of man that measures worth in terms of the amounts of goods and power one possesses, and on the other hand, he is commited to helping groups acquire these goods and powers they have been denied. It is, indeed, a philosophical contradiction and no amount of mental gymnastics can alter that fact.

The social interventionist views the problem of basic institutional change as necessarily involving conflict and organization. Conflict simply means that those who possess the power, those who have benefited most from the exploitation of others, should not be expected to either willingly or easily begin to share that power. Organization, on the other hand, implies that change only occurs when those who have been systematically prevented from gaining access to goods and power undertake a commitment to collective action based on an understanding of the forces which have kept them powerless in the past. The social interventionist believes in change from the bottom up, in the importance of consciousness-raising and understanding social contradictions as a part of the change process, and in the validity of group power and action as the basic vehicle for social and institutional change.

One final factor: for all his acceptance of the inevitability of conflict as an integral part of the change process, the social interventionist maintains the view that widespread disruption and violence need not accompany the basic alteration of social ideologies and institutional practices. The reasoning behind this belief is two-fold. First, the social interventionist does not see himself as necessarily working with one class, the most exploited. More often than not, the social interventionist focuses his attention directly on his own group, the middle class, hoping to broaden the basis of an eventual coalition. Second, the social interventionist believes that, when finally confronted with a strongly organized coalition which has demonstrated its ability to act in concert, those who have traditionally possessed the social power and economic resources will relinquish substantial control and seek a new form of accomodation. The social interventist accepts as an arbela of faith that the powerful will surrender some of their power in the interests of their own survival.

IV. The Social Revolutionary

Like the social interventionist, the social revolutionary is basically at odds with the fundamental assumptions under which most social institutions function. Unlike the social interventionist, however, the social revolutionary does not perceive the patient as salvageable. His analysis rests on the belief that historical imperatives are categorical in nature and do not include the possibilities of relatively peaceful transitions of power.

The social revolutionary approaches the problem of change from a position that stresses the unalterable opposition of social groups, whether sexual, racial, economic, or generational in nature. His focus, independent of the particular group with which he is associated, is to highlight the deficiencies that define that group's relationship to those who dominate the society. His goal is to increase the awareness of intergroup or interclass contradictions. This being the case, the social revolutionary deals less with the specific problems of improving concretely and immediately the plight of any one oppressed group. His is a commitment to revolutionary process, and intermediate solutions, unless they are related to that process, are perceived as either disruptive or interfering.

Like the social interventionist, the social revolutionary is caught on the horns of a dilemma, but the dilemma is of a somewhat different nature. To the degree that exploited groups act to improve the conditions under which they live, to that degree it is possible that there will be a significant decrease in revolutionary consciousness. As an example, witness the status of the trade-union movement in this country. But, on the other hand, for the social revolutionary to disengage himself from the efforts of the oppressed to garner a greater "share of the pie" is to condone, and perhaps facilitate, the continued subjugation of massive groups. As is the case with respect to the social interventionist, the dilemma has practical as well as philosophical implications.

As indicated at the beginning of this chapter, our primary purpose in trying to define oppression and social intervention was not to develop a common frame of reference. Rather, we have sought to establish and communicate a very particular stance toward both of these issues, the assumption being that the areas under discussion have already suffered too much from disingenuous attempts at creating an artificial sense of agreement.

As social scientists we are publicly committed to the search for truth. As human beings we are responsible for the specific truths we choose to guide us in daily life. By their very nature, the problems of oppression and social intervention cut across the usual and often comfortable distinctions we seek to make between our public-professional roles and our private-personal missions. We are now in a situation in which the truth-seeker ultimately becomes the subject of his own quest: we cannot claim immunity from ourselves.

2

The Making of a Social Interventionist

Social interventionists are not born, they are made. Unlike some athletes, creative artists, and others in whom there appears to have taken place a mystical process whereby genes and social destinies have been joined, the social interventionist is almost totally the product of his interactions with the environment. His vocation and often his entire existence are firmly embedded in the experiences and analyses of the settings and conditions in which the human drama is being played out.

Social interventionists are not what might be called "natural" people, that is, they neither blossom spontaneously nor do they appear to unfold gently as if guided by some quietly pervasive force ever responsive to the immutable laws of individual development. Rather, social interventionists surface, often with apparent reluctance, rarely without hesitation, and never unattended by more than a little doubt concerning the reasons for having "chosen" their peculiar vocation. And it *is* a peculiar vocation, for, unlike almost any other, there is no consensual agreement regarding their role, no institutional framework within which they can learn and perfect their skills, and no body of social support for the interventionist enterprise. Indeed, social interventionists are very "unnatural" people if by natural we mean those who both choose their profession from among existing or socially defined models and who then proceed along clearly marked routes to acquire the skills and experiences needed to become proficient.

If there is anything natural about the potential social interventionist, it is his inability to avoid becoming acutely aware of and deeply affected by the contradictions of the human condition. Moreover, the social interventionist, almost constitutionally, is incapable of remaining passive in the light of these experiences. Sooner or later he must act, and through these actions he makes clear his own guiding faith: *that there is an unalterable identity between his sense of incompleteness and the imperfections that define the human condition, especially as reflected in the existing relationships between people and the institutions or social processes which codify those relationships.*

The experiences that go into the making of a social interventionist are many and varied but, contrary to public mythology, only rarely are they of the "mind-blowing" variety. Dramatic, "one-trial learning" very infrequently characterizes the formative decisions by which interventionists become what they are. For every Moses who is suddenly and almost inexplicably transformed by a single violent act committed under the aegis of a Pharaoh, there are a thousand Cezar Chavez's who come by their interventionist stances only after repeated and painful personal experiences in the vineyards. For every John Kerry whose head has been "turned around" by the agonies of a Vietnam, there are a thousand

Malcolm X's whose lives offer mute testimony to the ravages of a system fast approaching complete madness.

In addition to the relatively few critical traumatic experiences that coalesce to produce the "interventionist decision," there are other factors which must be understood to appreciate the multiple routes and pathways which bring people to the interventionist camp. To begin with, it would be wrong to automatically assume that interventionists invariably spring from among the ranks of the oppressed. Indeed, it is frequently the case that social interventionists arrive at their new calling only after having been an integral part of the forces and groups they eventually come to oppose. Cyrus Eaton, for example, the man often referred to as the "communist-capitalist," was what some would call an oppressor long before he ever began to seriously question either the basis of his wealth or the discrepancies between his visions of the industrial enterprise and the conditions under which those who worked for him had to live. The Robert F. Kennedy who was summarily destroyed in a hotel kitchen in Los Angeles was a very different person from the one who sat behind Senator Joseph McCarthy during the days when a "point of order" signaled the imminent destruction of another reputation. In both examples we are confronted by significant changes in class allegiance and goals, and it may very well be that for some the experience and revulsion over having been a part of some exploiting group is an important precursor to the interventionist decision.

It should also be noted that the kinds of experiences out of which social interventionists are made do not invariably demand the direct participation of the individual. Often the eventual interventionist is little more than an observer of the human drama, cataloging and storing events until they can be integrated within a coherent conceptual framework to make sense of a host of apparently diverse and unrelated occurrences. Gandhi and Thoreau, for example, were acute and sensitive observers of the human condition, acting only after a period of reflection and drawing conclusions from their observations. The interventionist's formative experiences are not necessarily rooted either in a single class of events or in a particular kind of setting. Pete Seeger, for example, draws unto himself the essence of the interventionist's ethos from a continuing set of experiences spanning both years and continents. From the dustbowls of the Midwest to the Loyalist trenches in Spain, from the early and unpublicized days of the civil rights struggle to his most recent forays down the swells of the polluted Hudson River, Seeger's journey appears almost endless, unbounded by time and unlimited by place. He goes where the struggle takes him, continues to grow and change. Unless one wishes to interpret his behavior within some exceptionalist framework carefully reserved for latter-day Don Quixotes, one must assume that Seeger has evolved a conception of the human condition which sees common themes in the actions undertaken against Generalissimo Franco almost forty years ago and the skirmishes being waged today against the corporate destroyers of our environment.

Finally, the decision to become a social interventionist does not bring with it the need to abandon one's existing vocation. Neither does it invariably mean that one must disregard or deny one's previous training. Indeed, the opposite is much more often the case. Given that there really is no profession called social intervention, it should come as no surprise that most social interventionists already have a trade or are members of an existing professional group and that they continue their membership in these groups long after having assumed the interventionist stance. The consequence of having made the interventionist decision is not that one leaves one's craft, but that the focus and direction of one's activities within that particular profession change rather noticeably and, in most cases, irrevocably. For example, Ralph Nader continues to be identified with the legal profession, but it is clear that the nature of his commitment to the problems of consumer advocacy has markedly affected both the manner and content of his professional affiliation. For Martin Luther King, on the other hand, being a social interventionist brought with it the demand that he significantly broaden the scope and meaning of being a minister. By placing himself at the disposal of social history, King forged an unalterable alliance between his sermons in the church and his actions on the streets of America. And so it was that, when Martin Luther King languished in jail and perhaps even when he stopped the assassin's bullet on a terrace in Memphis, he was a minister, fulfilling his clerical responsibilities in what for him was the most profound and natural sense of the term. But it is also possible to remain a member of a profession and not try to broaden its definition or overly constrict it's focus and still be as one with the interventionist enterprise. In such instances one generally finds the social interventionist directing his energies toward problems of analyzing and exposing those practices, usually within his own profession, which perpetuate or reinforce the oppression of others. Within the author's profession, the helping professions, the work of William Ryan provides an excellent example. His book, *Blaming the Victim* (1971), is a probing analysis of the myriad ways in which the theories and practices of the social sciences have served to both legitimize existing social inequities and to prevent or at least seriously retard attempts to deal substantively with some of the more fundamental contradictions in our society. As such it constitutes a direct attempt at raising the consciousness of a particular group, the so-called liberal social scientific establishment. Thus, while Ryan's work is almost by definition restricted to his own profession, it is clearly the work of a social interventionist.

At this point let us pause for a moment and try to summarize our discussion. We have tried to describe the variety of routes which people have traveled to arrive at the interventionist camp. As we have tried to indicate, there is no profession labeled social intervention, and it should be clear

that what binds social interventionists together is much less
a factor of previous training than it is of current behaviors
and beliefs, irrespective of particular vocations. Put another
way, the unspoken bond that exists between Cezar Chavez,
a union organizer, Pete Seeger, a folk singer, and Ralph Nader, a lawyer, cannot be understood in terms of any formally
shared professional or preparatory experiences. There are
few institutional links between a migrant worker, a wandering activist, and a Harvard-educated lawyer. Nor are they
necessarily united by any common developmental experiences. For, unless one wishes to arbitrarily invoke "universal
developmental principles," such as psychoanalytically oriented stage theory, to "explain" their similarities, one would
be hard pressed to discover any common denominators between persons of widely differing class and caste. Rather, we
must look elsewhere for ways to describe, let alone understand, the forces which connect them. All we really know, or
that we can hypothesize, is that for all the important and
marked differences between them, they have achieved a common ground from which they appear to be trying to both deal
and have an impact upon the forces responsible for their initial separation. They seem to be bound by their analyses of
the present and their visions of the future. It is these analyses and visions, coupled with the behaviors they give rise to,
that place them in union with each other.

The making of a social interventionist, then, can best be
understood in terms of a *process* through which certain
classes of events become the experiential ground for subsequent social actions which, if not defined as "deviant," are
acknowledged to fall outside the mainstream of expected or
anticipated behavior. The process itself, while rarely smooth
or predictable, is punctuated by *specific experiences which
are no less socially salient than they are personally significant.* In other words, the referents go beyond the individual;
the events are almost always symbolic of larger issues and
social forces and consequently cannot be limited or fully

understood solely on the basis of individual dynamics. Their meaning lies somewhere else, beyond the protagonists in the immediate situation. The essential quality of these experiences, which it appears social interventionists cannot avoid perceiving, is that they mirror basic contradictions in society. They serve to highlight the persistent social inequites that exist between people and continually color their interactions.

More importantly, the experiences are ultimately placed in a kind of "institutional context" which functions to depersonalize acts of individual persecution. Thus, for example, the bestiality of one of the Pharaoh's soldiers, no different from the venom spewed by a white person trying to prevent a black child from entering a school classroom, is viewed within a framework of what might be called "systemic imperatives." While the individual act can never be condoned or pardoned, it is nevertheless viewed as a predictable event, as a necessary expression of the existing institutional arrangements under which people have been conditioned to respond in ways that continually demonstrate their mutual captivity. It was to this basic perception that Martin Luther King was responding when he made clear that his crusade against racism was as much concerned with saving the white man's soul as it was with insuring the survival of black people. For him, the analysis of the nature of bondage led to two inescapable conclusions: first, that the conditions under which exploitation took place were systemic in origin; and second, that oppressed people *and* their oppressors were at once both the victims and symbols of those systemic constraints.

Such an anlysis is the conceptual base of the social interventionist's stance in the world. For all the individual differences that exist between them, for all the different routes they travel, and for all the different ways in which they demonstrate their intentions, social interventionists are united by a common analysis of the human condition. In its simplest form it is an analysis which says that, so long as one person is not fully free, all people are part slave.

Critical Incidents:
Some Concrete and Personal Examples

The discussion so far has been necessarily abstract. By focusing attention on the phenomenological aspects of the process by which social interventionists are made, we have described some of the necessary conditions which comprise the experiences which ultimately characterize the emergence of individuals as social interventionists. In addition, we have conveyed a picture of the social interventionist not as a highly exceptional human being, but as an individual who perceives and responds to his environment in ways that are for him almost unavoidable. The discussion has had to remain rather abstract because we have been limited to using others as examples, interpreting motivations in an effort to arrive at what appear to be common dimensions of experience. It is time that we become somewhat more concrete.

This book, including this chapter, is not intended as an autobiography. There are several reasons for this, not the least of which being that I do not view my life as a matter warranting any undue public interest. Neither do I view my development as particularly inspiring or so potentially instructive to others as to merit much serious or close examination. Quite honestly, I believe that my life is really nobody's business but my own. Nevertheless, the overall purpose of this chapter is to describe the ground out of which the social interventionist emerges. Because we can only point with any certainty to our own experiences, it becomes important that I share with the reader those events which, from my point of view, are both personally siginificant as well as illustrative of the process by which an individual arrives at what we have called the stance of the social interventionist.

As the reader will see, the events to be described were hardly ever highly dramatic. Happily, perhaps, they never involved issues of life and death, for as has been indicated only rarely do dramatic experiences characterize the interventionist's evolution. Rather, they were almost always what might be called ordinary experiences, so apparently common in appearance as to seem unimportant. But, as I shall try to show, they were not. They formed a pattern and over a period of years gained in meaning and significance. Thus, each event became part of a process, linked to those which had preceded it and those which would follow. It is for this reason that I feel comfortable referring to them as "critical incidents," for each one, however apparently mundane, served to raise and intensify my awareness of the essential contradictions that define the human condition.

Example 1: The Statues

A situation becomes oppressive when an individual is forced to tolerate behavior in himself and others for which there is no legitimate rationale other than survival. It is a situation in which the oppressed individual, for reasons deeply rooted in fear, alters his or her customary behavior to face a threat which he or she has no power to control or change. The act is demeaning and there is a loss of integrity. Much like the professional waiter in one of Sartre's classic studies, the oppressed individual turns himself into an object, rendering himself empty and devoid of human choice. The situation is one in which, regardless of outcome, the individual always emerges with a bitter taste in his mouth, with the undeniable knowledge that his survival was at the expense of his humanity. Nevertheless, while involved in the situation, the individual says things that he doesn't mean, acts in ways that he doesn't feel, and endures behavior that on other days or under other circumstances he would find repugnant and unacceptable.

As a youngster growing up in New York, the first day of school was one of the very few educational events that I used to look forward to or anticipate with any degree of relish. In part, of course, this was because one could always count on meeting old friends or other kids with whom contact had been lost during those long, muggy, often empty days that marked our summers in the city. Mostly, however, I always looked forward to the first day of school because it afforded me the unique opportunity of quickly establishing my annual school identity—that of Class Clown. It always happened (at least from grades one through four) in the following way:

On the first day of school, after having lined up in "size places," having been marched off to class with one's designated partner and going through the ritualized attendance-card checking, the teacher would invariably write her name in bold letters on the blackboard. It was always a "she" in the lower grades. Then, almost as if playing out some unchanging scenario, the teacher would always say a few words about "getting to know each other" and immediately instruct us to get up when pointed to and "tell the class your name and what your father and mother do for a living." The teacher always managed to initially seat us in alphabetical order, leaving for later the question of seating changes necessitated by visual problems, hearing deficits, or the desire to separate troublemakers from their companions.

This was "It," the moment for which I had been waiting. Trying to contain my growing excitement, I would attempt to feign indifference as the Frankie Antonicks, Shirley Bloombergs, and Larry Fuscos dutifully rose to "share" with the rest of us their names, most of which we already knew, and what their parents "did for a living." We usually knew that too. Finally, it was my turn, and I remember jumping up as dramatically as possible to announce to the world that my name was Itzi Goldenberg, that my father was a barber, and that my mother was Fannie the Bloomer-Maker. It always worked. It brought the house down, unnerved the teacher, and invariably established my identity for the rest of the school year.

Well, even though my mother wasn't exactly a bloomer-maker, she worked for more than thirty-five years as a zig-zag machine operator in New York's garment district in a sweatshop that turned out women's underwear. For virtually all of those years she was a member of the ILGWU (the International Ladies Garment Workers Union) and she served as her shop's elected chairlady for close to fifteen years, collecting union dues and trying to help her co-workers take advantage of whatever benefits the union made available. She was a strong believer in collective bargaining and worked long and hard to insure the growth of Local 62 of the ILGWU.

But union or no union, work for a zig-zag machine operator was always seasonal with layoffs "just around the corner," generally occurring at some point either right before or just after Christmas. The season was from about April to December, and I remember well how my mother used to count up the number of weeks she had been working, hoping against hope that before she was laid off she could accumulate the thirty-nine weeks of work one needed in order to qualify for unemployment insurance.

The number thirty-nine became a magic number in our house. It symbolized stability and achievement, but more than anything else it represented a buffer for the days to come when the family would have to try to make it on my father's salary alone. Given the fact that my father, a barber, was never known as a particularly good provider, it was very important that my mother work at least enough weeks to guarantee the additional income from unemployment insurance that would later keep things together during the weeks of her enforced idleness.

My mother's boss, the owner of the factory, was a man whose name I alway thought appropriate to his countenance: Mr. Stern. My memories of him will always be those of a spindly little man continually darting up and down the rows of zig-zag machines, ever barking and goading the women to "hurry up and finish the order." He was a vile little creature and universally disliked by the workers. But he was also a powerful man, genuinely feared, a man who knew well the meaning of the magic number thirty-nine, and, consequently, a man on whose right side it was important to remain.

Mr. Stern, apparently fancied himself as a man of unlimited goodness, and instituted a practice whereby each year, generally around Thanksgiving time, his "married girls" were to bring one of their children to the shop to meet him. Being an only child, the "honor" for me was an annual one, and for several consecutive years I dutifully trekked by

subway from the East Bronx to the 28th Street Station of
the IRT, always bearing in mind my mother's admonition to
"be nice and talk clear to the boss."

Each year the routine was the same. I'd enter the
factory in the late afternoon, walk out on "the floor," and
make for my mother's machine. Immediately I'd be enveloped
by my mother and some of the women whose machines were
near hers, hugged, passed around, told how much I had
grown, and warned, in Italian, Spanish, and Russian, to be
worthy of my parents. My mother's eyes would sparkle. She
seemed genuinely proud.

Then, after no more than a few moments, it was time to
go and "say hello" to Mr. Stern. My mother would take my
hand and lead me up the aisle, being careful that none of the
leftover bits of material on the floor clung to my carefully
pressed corduroy pants. There at the end of the row, always
smiling and squinting at me, was Mr. Stern.

At that exact moment I would feel a gentle nudge on the
back of my neck as my mother urged me onward. I would
then extend my hand to the boss, smile as I had been
instructed to do, and say: "How do you do, Mr. Stern." Mr.
Stern would then bend over, grab me under the chin with his
thumb and forefinger, shake my head, and say: "Well sonny,
are you being a good boy, or has your mamma been lying to
me?" I would dutifully acknowledge that my mother wasn't
a liar and begin to brace myself for the scene that invariably
followed.

Mr. Stern, speaking loud enough so his voice almost
could be heard over the numbing din of the machines, would
tell me what a "good girl" my mother was, how she came to
work on time, and how much nicer she looked than the other
"Spics and Pollacks around here." I'd look up at my mother.
Her eyes no longer sparkled. They had a vacant look about
them, almost as if she were no longer behind them. But Mr.
Stern went on and on, his rasping voice blending in with the
incessant whirring of the machines. I tried to think only of
the machines, sit on my growing anger as my mother had
instructed me to do, or sink slowly into my favorite revery,
that of succeeding Phil Rizzuto as the next great shortstop
of the New York Yankees.

But the reveries couldn't last. Mr. Stern saw to that as he would put a proprietory hand around my mother's shoulders, give her a squeeze, and reiterate what a "good girl" she was and how I should "follow her good example and make her proud." My insides would churn. Who the fuck was this skinny little bastard? Who gave him the right to call my mother a "girl"? Shirley Bloomberg was a girl. She was ten years old. Yeah, she was a girl. My mother was all grown-up. She was a lady, not a girl. And who gave him the right to put his grubby hand around my mother? He wasn't family. Hell, he wasn't even a friend. If my father were here now, that son of a bitch Stern wouldn't dare to put his arm on my mother. And if he *did* try, he wouldn't use it again for a month. Again I looked up at my mother. She seemed to have turned herself into a block of stone, the only remaining part of her that was still alive rested quietly on my neck, gently kneading my anger, offering a kind of reassurance that couldn't be spoken.

Mercifully, the end was now in sight. After what seemed like an eternity, Stern's apparently endless monologue was approaching its predictable climax. With a last flourish of words, none of which I could any longer differentiate from the mass of sounds that had been punishing my ears, he would reach into his pocket, pull out a fifty-cent piece, and press it firmly into my hand. As abruptly as he had appeared, he was gone, leaving behind him the statue and her son. Wordlessly, my mother would turn away from me and I would follow her back to her machine. There was no more laughing, no more chatter, no more hugs from co-workers. Only the incessant sounds of the factory remained to remind us where we were and, even more importantly, who we were.

The trip back home was invariably a quiet one, and it almost seemed as if the clatter of the subway train somehow served to soothe my mother and ease her way back to me. Slowly she would begin to talk about something, usually supper, or perhaps how lucky we were to have gotten a seat at 86th Street. But, for me, there was still the churning in my stomach, the sight of Mr. Stern's arm around my mother's shoulders, the sounds of his words as they cascaded out of his mouth. I turned to my mother and asked her why Mr. Stern was the way he was and why she let him do "those things that he did." Again my mother seemed to become tense, and I thought for a moment that I could see the vacant look returning to her eyes. But it didn't return. Instead, she looked down at me, sighed deeply, smoothed back the hair that had fallen over my eyes, and told me that one day, maybe when I was older, I would understand.

Well, she was right. I think I finally understand.

Example 2: Wish You Were Here

The experience of powerlessness is perhaps the single most important feature linking oppressed people. To be unable to change the conditions under which one lives, to be rooted in soil from which there is no escape, is to be rendered impotent in the face of forces which become more and more anonymous as they become more and more arbitrary. Eventually one's own anonymity begins to rival that of the systems,' and the inability to act slowly transforms the individual into a passive and compliant being, a person ready to be manipulated at will. Whatever freedom remains is carefully reserved for those situations shared with others who are being exploited. This is one of the essential themes in Ralph Ellison's book, *The Invisible Man*. It is also the basic theme underlying much of the use of social science technology in American industry. At times, as in the example described below, the manipulation is crude and painfully obvious. At other times, particularly as technological sophistication increases, the process becomes more subtle and varied, filled with ambiguous nuances that becloud basic issues and increase distortion. In either case, however, the essential ingredient in the recipe is a captive audience, people already powerless and, therefore, readily available for experimentation.

It was a typical late-July day in New York. The temperature was in the nineties, the humidity nearly a hundred, and, even though it was almost suppertime, the sun hung in the sky as if it either had nowhere to go or no intention of ever leaving.

I was sitting alone in the kitchen of our three-room apartment. School was out. It was too hot even for a twelve-year-old kid to play ball, and the only way to try and keep cool was to sit in a darkened room and sip a homemade "egg cream," a combination of Hershey's syrup, milk, and seltzer. It was close to 6:30 P.M. and I expected my mother home at any moment. My father wouldn't be home for almost an hour.

The key turned in the lock, the door opened, and my mother came through the foyer and into the kitchen. Just by looking at her, I could tell that she probably hadn't had a seat during the rush-hour subway trip from downtown. Her clothes were riveted to her body as though they were part of her skin. Sweat poured from her forehead and formed little wet pools in the wrinkles and crevices around her eyes. When she moved even ever so slightly, she left in her wake the smell of clammy skin and stale Cashmere Bouquet powder. She was exhausted, and, it only being a Wednesday, I remember wondering how she'd make it through the rest of the week. She seemed to be moving in slow motion, and this, coupled with the lights being off, gave her an eerie, almost spectrelike appearance.

Although she saw me sitting near the table, she didn't bother to acknowledge my presence. Instead, almost as if completing some prearranged and overlearned ritual, she sat down, took off her shoes, and gazed silently out of the kitchen window and onto the courtyard beyond. After only a moment or so, she shook her head briskly as if to clear it, and got up. Still not having said a word to me, she went over to the stove, lit a match, and started a fire underneath an old kettle that always seemed to be filled with water. Then she took a tea bag and placed it in a large glass that stood near the stove. I remember thinking how strange my mother's ways were. Here it was, hotter than hell, but instead of making herself something cold to drink—if not an egg cream, at least some iced tea—she was going to drink hot tea from a glass. At any rate, while waiting for the water to boil, she sat down, took a napkin from the table, and started running it over her face.

At that point I really wanted to do something that would

make her feel better. She was obviously tired and weary.
And so, thinking that some music might help, I reached
around and turned on the radio. It took the radio a moment or
so to warm up, but soon the room began to be filled with
the dulcet sounds of Eddie Fisher singing *Wish You Were
Here.*

> They're not making the skies
>   as blue this year.
> Wish you were here.
> As blue as they used to when
>   you were near.
> Wish you were here.

My mother's head began turning slowly, becoming
oriented to the radio. Her eyes opened wide and I thought I
saw a strange look on her face.

> And the mornings don't seem
>   as new,
> Brand new as they did with
>   you.
> Wish you were here.
> Wish you were here.
> Wish you were here.

Suddenly she began to tremble, at first slowly, but then
more and more. Her face became pale and new beads of
sweat appeared on her forehead to take the place of those
she had just wiped away. She looked frightened, her eyes
darting around the room.

> Someone's painting the leaves
>   all wrong this year.
> Wish you were here.
> And why did the birds change
>   their song this year?
> Wish you were here.

Her trembling increased. First her head, then her hands,
finally her whole body. She put her fingers over her mouth
as if to stifle a scream and then she looked at me, stared at
me, and beyond me toward the radio. Something terrible was
happening to my mother. And it was happening right in front
of me.

They're not shining the stars
as bright
They've stolen the joy from
the night.
Wish you were here.
Wish you were here.
Wish you were here.

I looked around. It was the radio. It had something to do with the radio. But what? My mother's eyes were almost pleading with me now. What had I done? What could I do to fix things? The radio! Yes, the radio. That was it! I swung around in my chair and quickly turned it off.

The room was quiet and dark once more. Slowly, ever so slowly, my mother stopped shaking. Her face began to lose its tormented look, her hands dropped back into her lap, and it appeared as if all the energy that remained in her body slowly began to ease its way out. Her head sank and her shoulders soon followed, both seeming lured to a merciful relief. My mother was calming down. It was over.

Some time later, after having drunk her hot tea, she tried to explain things to me. It seems that a bunch of "nicely dressed professional men" had been brought into the factory by Mr. Stern. They had hooked up loudspeakers all over the floor where the zig-zag machine operators worked. And for the past ten days they had been playing *Wish You Were Here*. First, Eddie Fisher's rendition, then in cha-cha tempo, then with a merengue beat, in waltz time, or in boogie-woogie. *Wish You Were Here* coming at you from all sides, every second, every day. Sometimes the nicely dressed professional men would appear, ask how you liked one version compared to another, and count the number of slips or brassieres you had finished that morning. But day in and day out it was *Wish You Were Here*.

It was only years later that I fully understood what had happened. The industrial psychologists, the "time and motion boys," had been brought in. Using their expertise, the latest in scientific know-how, these forerunners of the organizational behavior people had turned the factory into an experimental laboratory. The workers were the subjects and the goal was clear : to increase production and profits. The woman who trembled on that hot summer evening was powerless to stop them. She became one of the numbers.

Example 3: Oh Boy, Ain't I Lucky

All routines are, almost by definition, lackluster affairs. But what generally differentiates the routines of oppressed people from those higher up in the social order is the sheer physical and spiritual toll that is extracted. Whatever humor one finds accompanying the routine is usually of the laughter through tears variety so well described by the Yiddish writer, Sholem Aleichem. By and large, however, the humor is fleeting and generally serves to highlight rather than ease the burdens of one's day-to-day existence.

I saw very little of my father for the first six or seven years of my life. Like the man in Morris Rosenfeld's poem, *My Son,* he would leave for work long before I awoke and would return at night only after I was already asleep. His routine never changed : gone by 6 :00 A.M. and rarely back home before 7 :30 P.M. Also, he had to work on Saturdays, thus further cutting down on our chances to see each other. He tells me that during those years he never left or returned from work without kissing me, and I believe him. But I have no memory of those kisses.

Sunday was my father's "day of vacation," as he called it. It was also our one chance to be together. Unlike my mother who seemed to be able to sleep late on those mornings when she didn't have to go to work, my father was so conditioned to rising at 5 :30 A.M. that he was always up at that time, even on his precious "day of vacation." However, unlike the other days of the week, he would steal over to my bed, gently rouse me, caution me not to make a sound ("don't wake momma"), help me get dressed, and take me out with him.

I remember well those Sundays. We would leave the house and stroll through the still-darkened streets to an all-night cafeteria called Messinger's. Once there, we would invariably get a table near the window looking out on Boston Road and my father would buy two hard rolls and butter, a cup of coffee for himself, and a glass of milk for me. Then we would sit quietly or talk for a long time. He would dunk his buttered roll in his coffee, tell me how Messinger's made the best coffee in the Bronx, and then, depending on how old I was, he would carefully measure out a few teaspoonsful of his coffee and pour it into my milk.

At about 8:00 A.M. we would leave Messinger's and, hand in hand, make our way to the Bronx Zoo, generally getting there just around the time it opened. I remember that my father loved the lion house and we always went there first. He would stand for a long time gazing into the cages that held the big cats. Occasionally, almost wistfully, he would remark how much better off the lions were than "working people." "What do they have to do all day," he asked. "Just sit in a nice warm place, eat good food, and maybe roar once in a while. Not such a bad life."

Eventually, maybe an hour later, we would leave and walk back home, making very sure that we were quiet when we entered the apartment "just in case momma's still asleep." The rest of my father's day off also followed a rather set routine, for regardless of whatever else happened, two things always stayed the same. In the early afternoon he would turn on the radio, press his ear close to the speaker, and listen to the Sunday Symphony on WQXR. After the symphony he would lie down on the couch that opened up to make my bed and take a nap before supper.

Many years later, when I was in my first year of college, I finally got to see the world as my father saw it every morning of his working life. It was January, exam time, and I had been scheduled to take one of my finals at eight o'clock in the morning. I decided that, rather than staying up until all hours of the night, I would leave the house early and get to school in time to do some last-minute cramming. I asked my father to wake me when he got up for work so that we could walk down to the subway together. We could go no further together than the subway station because we were headed in opposite directions.

The following morning he dutifully woke me at 5:30 A.M. We dressed in silence, gathered up whatever we needed, and left the house. As we hit the street my father hunched over, pulled up the collar of his coat, adjusted his earmuffs, and slowly started trudging his way up the block. He was in his early sixties then, and beginning to slow down noticeably.

It was a typical, miserable winter's morning, damp and grey and cold, with an icy wind biting through whatever you wore for protection. The streets were deserted and empty of life, the cold having driven even the ever-present alley cats to seek refuge elsewhere. But mostly it was dark. A pale moon was still out, a few stars could be seen, and only a glimmer of light way off in the distant sky marked the approaching dawn.

I decided it was probably time for some humor. I mean, hell, the hunched-over man walking next to me really looked about as miserable as the day was grey. So I nudged my father with my elbow and said: "Gee, papa, look at all the things you got going for you. I just can't get over it. I mean who else can go to work and have the moon, the stars, and the sun all at once? Like aesthetically, it's incredible. I never saw anything like it. Imagine that, papa. The moon, the stars, and the sun—all at the same time." My father said nothing. He just kept walking. But about a minute later he nudged me with his elbow, cocked his head in my direction, looked at me out of the corner of his eye, and said: "Oh boy, ain't I lucky."

Example 4: The Wandering Jew

The success of any exploitative system ultimately depends on the degree to which those who are exploited come to view and evaluate themselves in terms of the norms laid down by their oppressors. In psychoanalytic theory, the phenomenon of incorporating the values of the so-called enemy is called identification with the aggressor, and it signifies the developmental process by which attitudes concerning self-worth and social responsibility are acquired. Essentially, the process of identifying with the aggressor is complete when the vulnerable individual, the "object of abuse," succeeds in first introjecting and then claiming as his own the orientations of his "abuser." Whether one is referring to personal attitudes, for example, conceptions governing the acceptability or unacceptability of specific behaviors, or to broader issues which link the individual with cultural mystiques, such as conceptions about success, masculinity, femininity, or what have you, the importance of the process should not be underestimated. It often determines both the immediate efficacy of the system as well as its exploitative potential.

One of the most vivid recollections of my father is that of a man scurrying home from work. I see him darting his way through traffic, the electric leavings of the subway train showering him with a blanket of sparks as he feints and dodges his way across the wide street forever choked with cars, trolleys, and trucks. Hands in pockets, coat collar raised over his ears, avoiding at the last possible moment being struck by some vehicle, his daily negotiation of "the Avenue" was always cause for concern, not to mention wonder and gratitude at his survival.

My father's fondest hope was that one day my mother would be able to stop working. My mother shared that dream, and, as is still the case today among many poor people, women's liberation or no women's liberation, she longed for the day when she could finally stay home and do all the things she always wanted to do. She never specified what they were. My parents never realized that dream. Both of them had to keep on working until long after they qualified for Social Security.

During the last few years of my father's working life it became impossible for him to work a full day. The years of giving haircuts, of standing anywhere from twelve to sixteen hours a day, had taken its toll. He was in his late sixties by then, and physically unable to remain on his feet for a whole day. Much as he tried, he couldn't do it, and after much arguing and pleading, he finally agreed to work part-time. And so, he got a job on Times Square and 42nd Street, in a cut-rate barber shop located somewhere in the underground maze of midtown Manhattan. He called it a "*schlag* house," his term for a shop where haircuts cost only seventy-five cents and the emphasis was on the volume of business rather than the quality of the haircut. His working hours now were from 7:00 A.M. until about noon.

I was in graduate school at the time and no longer living in New York. One day I got a call from my mother. She was upset and said that my father was acting "peculiar," that he was never home when she got back from work at 6:30 P.M., and that he refused to talk to her about where he was spending the afternoons and early evenings. She asked me to come home. "You'll talk to him," she said, "and maybe he'll tell you what's the matter."

I came back home and tried to talk to my father, but he made it clear that he wanted no part of the conversation. When I persisted, he stormed out of the room, leaving my mother and me shaking our heads and looking bewildered. It just wasn't like him.

The next morning he prepared to go to work in his usual fashion. Before leaving the house he buttered a hard roll, carefully wrapped it in wax paper, and placed it in his coat pocket. Then he was gone, out into the still-darkened streets and off toward the subway. But this time he wouldn't be going to work alone. I had decided to follow him and find out what was going on.

After waiting until I was sure he was out of the building, I left to pursue my father.

It was, for the most part, an uneventful pursuit. He boarded the subway, got a seat, and dozed for a good while. Then, almost as if guided by some mysterious internal clock, he awoke a station or two before Times Square, got up, and moved toward the door. After leaving the train he made his way through the station, bought himself a container of coffee, and entered the barber shop shortly after 7:00 A.M. After nodding to a few of the other workers, he took off his coat, donned a greyish smock, took a sip of his coffee, and went over to his chair, one of eight chairs lined up facing a mirror that extended almost the entire length of the store.

From about 7:15 A.M. until his quitting time shortly after noon he stood behind his chair giving haircut after haircut. There seemed to be no dearth of customers. Men sat in a long row of chrome-plated chairs, some patiently, others impatiently, awaiting their turn. Each "cut-rate special" took about ten minutes and the entire operation had an assembly-line air to it. Periodically, while one customer was leaving and another prepared to take his place on the chair, my father would take a bite of his buttered roll and another sip of coffee. There was little of the supposedly customary talk between barber and patron. It was all business, continuous silent movement.

Shortly after noon my father stopped. After carefully putting away his tools, he took off his hair-speckled smock, shook it briskly, and hung it up. Then, nodding once more to the barber working at the chair next to him, he put on his coat and left the shop.

After leaving the store he went up the stairs to 42nd Street. As always Times Square was a mass of colors and movement. People scurried past one another, each one propelled by some unfathomable private mission. Rows of all-night movies, clothing stores, luncheonettes, and souvenir tourist traps dotted both sides of the street. Music spewed out of the penny arcades, loud, pulsing, nerve-racking. But my father seemed oblivious to it all. Instead, he made his way directly to a Horn & Hardart's Cafeteria.

Once inside the huge restaurant he bought himself another club roll and a cup of coffee, and sat down at a table near the window. For a long time he nursed his coffee and stared out the window at the constantly shifting but never-changing scene outside. Occasionally he stretched his feet or rubbed his eyes. But mostly he just sat.

After about an hour, the coffee and roll by now long gone, my father got up to leave. Upon leaving Horn & Hardart's he walked slowly up the street, stopped at the corner newsstand to get himself a copy of *The Freiheit*, a Yiddish daily newspaper, and went straight down the stairs to the subway station. Again he got on the train and easily found a seat. Since it was only about 1:30 P.M., not rush hour, seats were plentiful. The train took off, my father read his newspaper, and it seemed as if the trip back home had begun. But then the "peculiar things" started happening.

When the train pulled into our station my father didn't get off. Instead, he remained where he was, glanced around, and went back to his reading. Only at the next stop did he get up and leave the subway. Once outside, he descended the stairs to the street, and now, walking very rapidly and with apparent purpose, he made his way across the street, up a hill, and into a small park in this neighborhood that was clearly not "ours."

The park was almost deserted. A few people sat in the wooden benches that dotted the area, but the chilly, grey, late-autumn weather had apparently discouraged others from venturing out. A few brittle brown leaves whipped by, swirled about by a wind whose direction seemed to change from moment to moment. The park was as bleak as the people who inhabited it and the day which enveloped it.

My father sat for a long time, his coat collar pulled up over his ears and his hat pulled down over his forehead. Occasionally he'd stir, change his position, or bury his hands deeper in his pockets. But mostly he just sat.

After a long time—it was now about 4:00 P.M—he got up and began walking around. He circled the park a couple of times and then slowly made his way up a small side street and toward a diner that stood at the far corner. When he got to the diner he went in, seated himself at the counter, and ordered another cup of coffee. Again he sat for a long time toying with the cup in front of him. And, as if to further guarantee his already perfect anonymity, he pulled out his newspaper; placed it before him, and used it to shield himself from the other lone customer in the diner.

It was now somewhat past 5:00 P.M. and the diner began filling up with people on their way home from work. My father got up, paid for his coffee, and left. He then made his way back to the park, back to the bench he had been sitting on almost two hours before. It was still empty and so he sat down once again. It was even chillier now than before. The wind whistled past him and a lone dog, skinny and sick-looking, briefly sniffed at his shoes before slouching back and limping his way across the park. My father hunched his shoulders, moved his body deeper into the contours of the bench, and remained sitting quietly.

Finally, at about 6:30, he got up to leave. Slowly he made his way through the park, down the hill, and across the street to the subway station. Mounting the stairs, he pulled a token from his pocket and inserted it into the turnstile at the entrance to the platform. A train was pulling into the station as he walked out on the ramp. The doors opened and he entered quickly. One stop later, at "our" station, he left the train and made his way down to the street.

In his usual fashion, he scurried across the congested avenue, hands in pockets, feet picking their way adroitly through the mass of human and nonhuman traffic. It was about 7:00 P.M. now, and the streets were filled with people returning from work. Once in a while he would nod to someone or lift his hand in recognition as someone else passed by him. It seemed as if the streets were filled with familiar faces, and, although greetings took place silently, almost perfunctorily, it was clear that the people were not strangers to each other. They were all connected in some fashion: the wordless street drama was an intimate part of whatever they shared.

In a little while my father was home. I entered the house soon after.

Later that evening, long after supper was over, I confronted my father with what had happened. I replayed his day for him, complete with all the details and nuances I could remember. At first he was furious with me. "Who the hell are you?" he asked, "The F.B.I.? My own F.B.I.?" But his anger was fleeting, almost empty, more a formality than an exercise in genuine passion. Soon he grew silent, his eyes gradually filled, and a tear worked its way down his cheek. He put his hand to his face, lowered his head, and wept.

We held each other for a long time. There was nothing to say. We both knew. And so we just held each other and let our tears wash the years away.

Later we spoke again. We spoke in Yiddish because it was easier. My father knew quite well what he was doing, why he was wandering around all day in some strange neighborhood so that he could arrive back home "on time like the other workers." As he put it, it would be "a shame and an embarrassment" for people to think that Nathan Goldenberg couldn't work a full day anymore.

I countered with all the "right arguments." I reviewed for him how, as one of the people who helped organize the barbers union in New York, he had always spoken of the dignity of work and had fought for workers' benefits so that when they were too old to work they could retire without loss of respect or honor. I threw up to him his own and oft-repeated disdain for the ways in which Americans had been taught to gauge success, define manhood, or understand worth.

But he knew all that, knew it only too well. And I knew that I too was talking without conviction. Finally he looked at me and said: "I know it all. I even still believe it all. But in the end they get you. The years tear your words up and the pain tears your mind up. And that's how they get you. Little by little they make you choke on yourself. You finish up feeling the opposite of what you really are. That's how they win. They turn you inside-out and upside-down. You see son? Now I'm inside-out and upside-down."

We have tried in this chapter to describe the process by which social interventionists become what they are. Starting with the premise that only rarely is one born to be a social interventionist, we have tried to define the conditions and experiences which enter into the making of such people. Far more often than not, the clay out of which the social interventionist is molded is dull grey in color, devoid of sparkle and brilliance. Like all clay, it hardens slowly and with little accompanying fanfare. But harden it does until it eventually stands solid and unyielding, forever brittle but nonetheless formidable.

Independent of how they get there, however, social interventionists create a world for themselves, a world characterized by personal visibility, public risk, and unselfconscious partisanship, the kind of partisanship that is both scornful of neutrality and suspicious of compromise. Moreover, it is a world bordering on absolutes, where "winners" and "losers" are willingly pitted in battle, the ultimate outcome of each struggle being an incremental but concrete, observable, and measurable shift in power and resources. It is a Right Now! world, forever restless, often chaotic, and very rarely tender.

3
Understanding the American Experience

More often than not, moves by specific groups to protest or correct longstanding and amply documented social inequities appear as singular explosions of energies that have become focused and transformed into action. A part of a ghetto is burned down; acrimony marks the attempt by community groups to gain greater control over their children's education; a boycott draws attention to the existence and desperation of the migrant worker; and place names like Wounded Knee, Watts, Kent State, Oceanhill-Brownsville, and Attica flash before a seemingly always startled public. News of these events blaze for a few frightening or inspiring moments and then quickly vanish amid calls for "restraint" and "patience" with the promise of reassessments and attempts to once again investigate and analyze the many supposed "root causes" of each outburst. In every instance the institutional response to the crisis betrays a singular unwillingness to understand either the festering process behind each event or the essential interrelationships of the events themselves. Rather, what is communicated to the broad "unaffected" public is a double message: first, that the particular explosion in question is an incredibly complex affair, a problem of multiple dimensions and numerous perspectives; and second, that the outburst is an isolated event and, therefore, essentially unrelated to other happenings involving other groups, times, and places.

Actually, the event usually is neither difficult to understand nor easily disassociated from other events. Societies do not operate according to tables of random numbers. There is lawfulness in the social arrangements under which people live, a set of regularities that serve to both mask and articulate the overall sweep and direction of events. Events may appear to occur haphazardly, to be the products of chance, and to have few if any historical antecedants. Certainly there are times when this is the case. Most often, however, it is not. Like any well-constructed symphony, a social system is composed of recurring patterns, modulations, transitions, and codas, all of which are interconnected, unified around a central and relatively unchanging theme. The theme organizes events along dimensions that are as purposeful as they are predictable. The problem then, especially for those engaged in social intervention, is to discover and isolate this basic theme, to trace its undulating presence through its myriad peaks and depressions.

In this chapter a vantage point will be presented from which it becomes possible to understand social unrest without continually resorting to the tendency to seek an exotic explanation for each outburst. What is needed is a reasonably clear and simple way of describing the "American experience" and of conceptualizing the forces that shape and define that experience. The ultimate significance of such a conceptual model will more than likely depend on the appropriateness with which it can be used to systematically organize heretofore apparently diverse sets of data. For the present, however, our concern is with uncovering the basic theme around which the social interventionist must weave effective variations.

America I:
Values, Assumptions, and People

As in all societies, the American scenario operates according to the notion that its citizens should be both bound by and commited to certain objectives. Over time, these personal and social goals attain the status of *values*, and are imbued with all the meaning, mystique, and significance that usually attends the elevation and eventually the transformation of discrete human activities into cultural imperatives. One's ultimate worth as a human being, at least in societal terms, is judged with respect to the degree to which one is perceived as both mirroring and attaining these values.[1] What differentiates one society from another is not the absence of values and their accompanying cultural "press," but the particular values that are defined as intrinsic to the human condition.

We might begin by asking the reader to visualize American society as an imperfect hourglass (see Figure 1), with the bottom part significantly larger than the portion on top. The upper portion represents those core values which our society defines as crucial to its identity, consistent with its historical mandate, and essential for the experience of fulfillment on the part of its people. *Stripped of all accompanying rhetoric, these values revolve around the attainment of goods and power.*[2]

At the base of the hourglass are the people—all the people, regardless of class, race, sex, or age—and at least in theory the model is one of people striving to gain access through a hypothetical "access channel" to the goods and power they have been conditioned to accept as indicative of both self-worth and social meaning.

Figure 1. The Basic Model

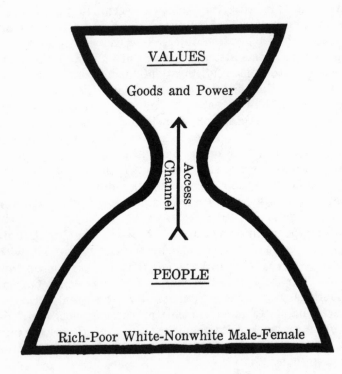

Before proceeding any further, however, it would be well to define more clearly exactly what is meant by the terms "goods" and "power." Goods simply refer to those material things that both guarantee survival and, if possessed in sufficient amounts, can be utilized to significantly ease the burden of one's existence. In theory as well as in ·practice the more goods an individual possesses, the less time he must devote to the problems of basic survival, and consequently the more energy he can employ to pursue the particular drummer whose tune has fallen upon his receptive ear. Goods can be money, property, or any other tangible social commodity that carries with it an agreed-upon value and can be converted, bartered, or otherwise transformed into alternate forms of resources. Power, on the other hand, is the ability to control or influence directly or indirectly the conditions under which one lives. To be empowered is to be able to exercise specific leverage over events that impinge themselves on one's existence; to have power is to have access to those resources which can be employed to either reduce one's feeling of discomfort or increase one's sense of dominion. *Goods and power are, in short, the stuff out of which survival is either transformed into a full-time career or relegated to a part-time activity.*

There was nothing accidental about depicting the upper portion of the hourglass, encompassing goods and power, as much smaller than the lower section. The American ethos is predicated on the existence of a number of crucial assumptions about those things it values the most. Indeed, it is possible to begin to understand both our nation's history as well as the manner in which the "system" currently operates by first stating and then critically analyzing the implications of the assumptions traditionally made about goods and power in this country. Simply put, these assumptions are that:

1. *Goods and power are not, either by definition or by their nature, limitless. They are entities to be viewed and treated as ultimately both finite and non-recoverable.*

2. *Whatever goods and power exist at a particular point*

will, under no conditions, be shared equally among the people.

3. *It is the individual who is the major referent for any and all analyses concerning the manner in which goods and power are both acquired or not acquired and used or misused.*

In a very real sense the assumptions listed above, especially when taken together, provide the intellectual and perhaps the spiritual basis for the development of a socioeconomic system which of necessity must be *exploitative* in nature. It is a system where one person's advantage ultimately depends on another's disadvantage, where one person's success must be predicated on another's failure, and where one person's rise must occur at the expense of another's decline.[3] In addition, it is a system which must be *competitive* in nature, for, whether or not it is indeed true that goods and power are inherently finite, the assumption that resources will not be shared virtually guarantees the emergence of a singularly competitive mentality. What is perhaps most intriguing about the assumptions is the initial illusion they create about the intrinsic equality among the people of the existing social system. By making the individual the sole analytical referent, by focusing almost exclusively on the individual as the principal actor in the unending drama of survival and transcendence, a scenario is created whereby "success" and "failure" need never be thought of in terms beyond personal capacity, energy, motivation, and luck. If it is logical to assume that a system predicated on assumptions leading to exploitative and competitive behavior is, ipso facto, an *"oppression-inspiring" system,* then the final assumption of individualism serves to make it appear that the resulting oppression is not systematic either in nature or by intent. In theory it is only individuals who can oppress or be oppressed; group or class oppression is, by design, an assumptive impossibility. That this assumption is not true should go without saying, and we shall return to this issue later in this chapter. For the present, however, it is important that we understand the assumptions in their own light and on their own level. It is for this reason that we drew the hourglass the way we did; that is to say, with *all* the people starting out at the same point.

In partial summary, then, the basic model is an apparently simple one. We are a people for whom the acquisition of goods and power has become synonymous with the demonstration of self-worth. Our acceptance of the presumed identity between goods and power and the meaning of our existential passage has elevated them and the quest to attain them from the realm of mere activity to the status of a cultural imperative. Now, as social values, they both define and dominate the manner in which we assess ourselves and our relationships to others. The system, such as it is and by virtue of the assumptions it makes about goods and power, is one which inspires oppression, a system in which exploitation and competition emerge as among the most "reasonable" ways of dealing with the world and other human beings. The model is one which envisions everyone as starting out at some relatively low point without power or goods, battling his or her way up through the access channel, and striving to amass a modicum of material wealth and influence. Because of the assumptions about the scarcity and nonsharing of the existing goods and power, the process of pursuit creates a bottleneck which results in individuals either making it through or falling back as a direct consequence of their own talents, efforts, and luck.

America II: Media, Myths, and Institutions

Of course, the model is really not as simple as it initially appears to be. With an overabundance of people constantly vying for an assumedly finite amount of goods and power, it becomes imperative that the system develop mechanisms whereby it can accomplish maintenance of the myth of its essential "openness" and control the overall number and speed

Figure 2. The Differentiated Model

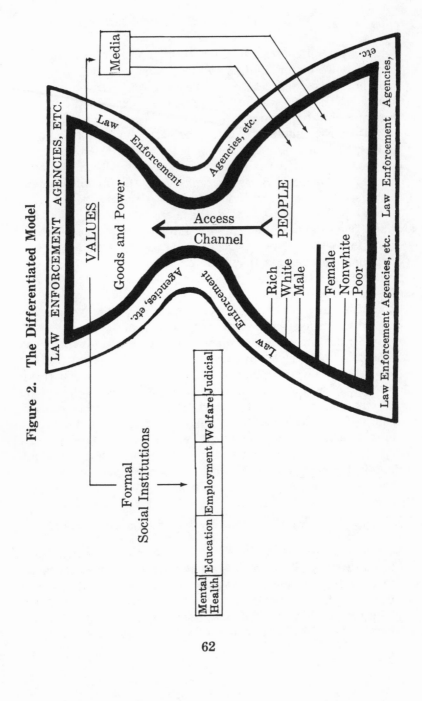

62

with which people gain access to the system's rewards and resources. In addition, as is the case in any society, there is the need to maintain order and continuity, to both set and enforce the limits of tolerable behavior. As indicated in Figure 2, the hourglass becomes more complex, but its basic structure remains unchanged.

In Figure 2 are represented the forces that combine to determine to a significant degree the overall manner in which the system operates. It is crucial that we understand these forces for they constitute the essential context within which individuals and groups are expected to strive to achieve stability. For purposes of clarity we will focus attention on three of these forces, the media, myths, and formal social institutions, and trace the manner in which they mediate interactions between people and the assumptive bases of the system of which they are a part.

Let us start with the *media*. It is essential that the values that dominate a society's "world view" be transmitted both continually and efficiently to all of its people. From the moment of birth, citizens must be exposed to the specific message around which they will be expected to organize their lives and through which they will develop the criteria for assessing self-worth. In a very general sense, at least in our society, the responsibility for delivering that message rests with the *media. By the term media, we mean the many and varied ways employed to convey the social "signal" that goods and power are the most important factors in life.* Whether it is through the written word, the legends and fables that are passed on from generation to generation, or the impressive arsenal that constitutes contemporary electronics technology, the signal must be transmitted. The senses must be filled to overflowing and the message learned and overlearned until it becomes an integral part of the person. In story and in song, through radio and television, via billboards and ballads, or by whatever means our fantasies and realities become separated, then joined, then separated again, the signal flows. Much as Hebb (1949; 1958) described the development of a "cell assembly," the twin values of goods and power require constant repetition for their successful implantation. Naturally, the most efficient pathway will vary with the particular level of development of the human receiver, so that certain vehicles for transmitting the message will take precedence over others at different points. The sights and sounds will change, the intensity and directness of the communication will be altered, its degree of differentiation will wax and wane, but the essential meaning and intent of the signal will remain solid and unyielding: it is toward goods and power that we go.

If there is anything that characterizes the message, it is the absolutely democratic manner in which it is delivered. Unlike the assumptions concerning goods and power (that they are both finite in amount and under no conditions to be shared equally among all the people), the message offered by the media is available to everyone in the same manner and with virtually the same intensity. There is, apparently, no limit to the message; neither are there any restrictions placed on its dispensation. It is available to all regardless of race, religion, or country of national origin. It is truly the most just of all commodities: it is forever blind to differences in class, color, age, or sex.

So much for the media and the ways in which people come to learn the values that underlie the system. But what about the people themselves, those who have accepted the message and all it implies about the human condition? It is here that we must turn to the basic *myth* that invariably accompanies the message.

Simply put, a myth is an invented story which attempts to account for something in nature. It is an assessment or interpretation of reality which, regardless of how powerful it appears, or how comfortable it makes certain people feel, or even how dominant a force it becomes in fictionalizing causality, is still basically either invalid or unsupported by accompanying data. *The basic myth in our society is that the "goods and power message" rains down upon the ears of people who will both start their quest from positions of comparable weakness or strength and have an equal chance of gaining access to the goods and power they have been taught to covet.*

That message, of course, is wholly untrue. Not all the people are poised and ready to begin the heralded race from the same point on the starting line. The race is fixed. Most of the horses are handicapped, long since having been weighted down in ways that make them long shots in the upcoming "Run for the Roses," the scamper for riches and influence. The intent of the myth is simple: to reinforce the notion of the individualistic thesis and to erase or otherwise mute the reality that whole groups of people, indeed the majority, have already been rendered "inoperative" by the time the message reaches them.

It is important to understand that these handicaps which render people inoperative have nothing to do with individual talent, intelligence, and motivation. That is the major point. Impressions to the contrary, a system which inspires oppression such as our system cannot be explained or understood on the basis of *individual* oppressors and oppressed *individuals*. Oppression is not a one-time affair in which the slate is rubbed clean upon completion of the act. It is both additive and cumulative in nature, as well as being transferable over time and across generations. It is mischief-making to persist in thinking that the children of people oppressed at Point A have the same chance of success at Point B (the time they enter the race) as do the children of parents who were not oppressed or not oppressed to the same degree. Oppression brings with it its own peculiar legacy, and this legacy is not automatically renegotiable nor can it be magically voided by its unwitting recipients. While it is still perhaps possible to accept, at least philosophically, the "tabula rasa" conception of man which suggests an equality of development based on individual potential, it would be unwise to assume such a stance when the issue becomes one of assessing the existence of realistic social options. As far as the offspring of the oppressed are concerned, the sins that have been visited upon their fathers and mothers become the functional ground out of which their own lives must grow. That ground is certainly far removed from the mythical starting point that is supposedly shared by all.

Having rejected the notion of Social Darwinism as a way of understanding differential individual success in our society, there is still the problem of accounting for how whole groups of people are rendered inoperative and why, in our society, those groups have traditionally been comprised of people who are poor, nonwhite, and female. In part, of course, such an analysis requires a historical and economic perspective which we do not possess. For example, the systematic exclusion of black people in this society can never be fully understood until one comes to grips with the economic basis of slavery. Consequently, our appraoch to the problem would have to begin by once again focusing attention on the fundamental assumptions around which the system itself is organized. Given the prevailing assumptions of scarcity and nonsharing with respect to material goods and social power, we already have indicated how generally exploitative and competitive behavior emerges as the most "appropriate" way of negotiating one's passage through the hypothetical morass of surging bodies. Such behavior does not occur, even initially, in a vacuum unaccompanied by consolidating tactics or unaided by prior advantages. The early settlers, for example, however currently ennobled for their heroism in escaping religious persecution, brought with them the conceptual and spiritual baggage which guaranteed the reemergence of a society based on class and caste. Their consciousness already was steeped in the exploitative ethos and their future would be one of changing the players, not the game. Thus, when our society is called "oppressive," it is not individuals who are being labeled. Similarly, references to the "classist," "racist," and "sexist" nature of our society become empty phrases when restricted to analyses of individual events. Rather, what we must come to grips with is the reality that *any* system predicated on the assumptions upon which ours is based must create victims. All discussions, however interesting, concerning which particular group is the most victimized can only lead to an embarrassing obfuscation of the basic issue.[4] Suffice it to say that for historical reasons, including the institutional dynamics associated with the acquisition, retention, and transfer of resources, entire groups have been either virtually excluded or seriously handicapped in the pursuit of goods and power. These groups include the poor, the nonwhite, and the female. It is this reality that is reflected in the reordering of the people represented in Figure 2. While all of the people receive the same message, they do not all begin their journey from the same place. Rich people, white people, and males, while theoretically as lacking in goods and power initially as poor people, nonwhites, and females, are, in reality, in a much preferred position. Theirs is the legacy of advantage in a society which denies the existence of such legacies.

We come now to the question of the role played by *social institutions* in the overall social matrix (see Figure 2). According to the present schema, *social institutions can be defined as those formal, public, and sometimes private settings whose primary responsibilities revolve around the tasks of both socializing citizens and facilitating or inhibiting their access to the goods and power they (the people) have been taught to covet.* Social institutions mediate the process which ultimately determines whether or not individual and group striving will come to fruition. They can be viewed as settings which, depending on how they define their mission, significantly influence the ease or difficulty with which people negotiate their passage through the system. As individual institutions they vary with respect to the particular areas in which their impact can be felt. For example, one can view educational settings as different from mental health agencies, and both as having a somewhat different focus from other formal social institutions, such as the employment subsystem, welfare agencies, and the judicial subsystem, that regulate behavior. Collectively, however, the social institutions, as Greenlee (1973) puts it, "control the treadmill"; it is their task to decide who makes it through the access channel and who does not.

Formal social institutions derive their power from a variety of sources including tradition, legislation, and the continuing and growing influence of an increasingly deified professional establishment. They exercise their leverage through the legitimizing and credentialing functions they perform. Both directly, through specific decisions concerning individuals, and indirectly, by being in the position to define the criteria around which legitimizing decisions are made, social institutions control the absolute dimensions of the access channel and the number and speed with which people are admitted or barred from the crucial passageways which ultimately separate the haves from the have-nots. Like Solomon, they must make decisions of immense importance in the lives of untold numbers. Unlike Solomon, however, as we shall indicate, their wisdom is more than a little suspect.

A culture's socializing and legitimizing institutions do not do their thing in a vacuum. Their legitmacy and their very existence depend on the degree to which they mirror and perpetuate the core values that lie at the foundations of the society they represent. Consequently, if the cultural imperative revolves around the issues associated with goods and power, and if acquiring goods and power requires learning and acceptance of an exploitative and competitive view of humanity, then the social institutions must themselves be reflective and supportive of that overall *Weltanshauung*. To retain their validity and to fulfill their destinies, courts, schools, and mental health, employment, and welfare institutions must wittingly or unwittingly become the handmaidens of the prevailing social ethos. Most importantly, if the results of history, intent, and chance have combined to produce a society whose oppressive fabric depends upon the systematic exclusion of certain groups because of class, race, or sex, then the responsibility for guaranteeing and masking reality falls upon the social institutions. Consequently, it should come as no surprise to find that *in each formal social institution whose functions in one way or another directly influence the passage of people through the system, we discover the same groups being put upon or otherwise detoured from full participation in the accepted existential struggle.* Poor people, people of "color," and females continually emerge as the victims of whatever policies and practices dominate the day-to-day decisions of our major social institutions. The pattern is simple, complete, and so consistent across institutions as to defy any interpretations predicated on the acceptance of chance as the appropriate explanatory principle. If the entire educational system is suspect, its effects are particularly devastating on the poor, the nonwhite, and the female (Fuchs, 1968; Rosenthal & Jacobson, 1968; Stein, 1971). If there is a question about the overall utility and effectiveness of the mental health professions, there are no questions concerning their counterproductivity with respect to the problems of the disadvantaged (Albee, 1959; Reiff, 1966; Chesler, 1973). If employment is an issue for people as a whole, it is a crisis for poor whites, blacks, women, Chicanos, and Indians (U.S. Department of Labor, 1970; 1971). If there are widespread concerns over the meaning and intent of social welfare, there is only the reality of its pulverizing effect on those who are forced to receive it in order to survive (Elman, 1966; Cloward & Piven, 1971). And if the administration of justice is a matter of general public concern, its misadministration is a matter of historical fact to those who possess neither money, connections, nor the "right" pigmentation.

But again, it would be a mistake of immense proportions for the reader to interpret the above as indicating the existence of a conscious and well-thought-out plan on the part of our social institutions to systematically discriminate against certain groups. To be sure, there are undoubtedly untold numbers of cases in which the destruction of souls can be traced to the invidious machinations of selected individuals and their venal associates (Patterson & Conrad, 1950; Zeiger,

1960; Ginzburg, 1962; Wechsberg, 1968). But to be seduced into focusing attention on specific outrages would be akin to missing the proverbial forest for the trees. The basic point in not that our formal social institutions are elitist, racist, or sexist, but that given their place and role in the social order they cannot easily be anything else. Their job is to validate existing social prophecy, not to change it.

Finally, let us consider the manner in which the system is kept intact. The responsibility for preserving the social order, for holding it in check, has traditionally fallen upon those identified with law enforcement. In our society this means the police and all associated agencies, both federal and nonfederal, whose mandate revolves around the day-to-day maintenance of domestic tranquility. They have the problem of dealing with the kind of behavior deemed disruptive or interfering with the "normal" conduct of everyday affairs. They are not responsible for defining the limits of acceptable behavior although in some instances they actively seek to assume such responsibilities. Defining behavioral limits is, by and large, the function of the formal social institutions. Neither are law enforcement agencies empowered to modify or in any other manner change the substantive context within which the system's affairs are regulated. As indicated in Figure 2, the law enforcement agencies can be viewed as the social *mechanisms* whose primary purpose is to surround the system they have been empowered to protect. As "preservative agents," their role is an instrumental one: to guarantee the kind of stability that is required for the system to function effectively and with a minimum of unanticipated or unmanageable interruption.

America III: The Machine at Work

Up to this point we have described three ideas: first, the assumptive themes around which the American experience is woven; second, the general consequences of these themes with respect to the development of an oppression-inspiring social fabric; and third, the particular institutional supports, mechanisms, and myths that, in combination, perpetuate and "validate" those themes. In addition, we have directed attention away from the tendency to impute evil to selected individuals and, instead, to focus a more critical awareness on the social imperatives that invariably accompany the elaboration of systems based on exploitation. Finally, we have provided an overview of the process by which groups are systematically excluded from the normative culture.

With that as the prologue, let us now describe, perhaps a little more concretely, exactly how the machine works its particular form of magic on those it has deemed expendable. Focusing attention on the formal social institution of which the author is a part, the mental health establishment, we shall depict the ways in which the helping professions interface with the strivings of the oppressed and how these efforts are blunted. The intention is not to heap unnecessary abuse upon any one social institution, but to try to increase our consciousness of the relationship between the orientations and practices of the mental health professions and the underlying assumptions of the system of which they are an extension and for which they perform a socializing and legitimizing function.

The scenario begins (see Figures 1 and 2) with everyone receiving the same goods and power message from the variety of transmission mechanisms available to the society. But, as we have previously indicated, most of the people receiving the signal have been handicapped for reasons including but not limited to historical accident and pernicious intent. All myths to the contrary, most of those receiving the signal, particularly the poor, the nonwhite, and females, will rarely attain a level of material and social comfort that is really different from that granted their parents.

Nevertheless, let us assume that, at least at the beginning of their journey, the expendables step off no differently from those whose trek through the system will be easier and ultimately more fruitful. The expendables embark with whatever sense of anticipation one might assume accompanies the initiation of a personally significant and socially sanctioned adventure.[5] Sooner or later it becomes obvious that something is drastically wrong, that the road is neither paved with good intentions nor is the traveler getting anywhere as a consequence of his/her efforts. The traditional confluence of vested interests and institutional forces coalesce to undermine the process of "making it." More and more of the traveler's time is devoted to the problems of survival; less and less energy, physical or psychological, is available to deal with questions of meaning or choice. Gradually the cumulative effects of limited options and misguided effort take their toll. The disparity between one's own condition and the condition to which one was impelled to aspire merely serves to intensify the emptiness of the original promise. Ultimately, with the steady decline of hope, there remains only the gnawing reality of an unlived and unlivable life. The initial struggle is over.

So where are we, particularly with respect to the dynamics outlined in Figure 2? We are in a situation in which the person who begins his journey with little chance of ever succeeding, essentially winds up at a point well below the access channel. The amount of accrued power and goods he has is so small as to virtually guarantee a future devoid of possibilities, a future devoted almost exclusively to the problems of basic survival.

It is at this juncture, when the reality of failure finally settles in, that two questions surface for discussion: first, what realistically are the options available to the embattled individual; and second, what traditionally has been the response of the helping professions to those options? In the pages that follow we shall explore these questions.

Option 1-Response 1:
The Encouragement and Facilitation of Adjustment.

For many, perhaps the majority of those whose basic expendability is finally driven home to them, the demise of the dream is not accompanied by any relief from what Davis (1971) calls "the overall scenery of oppression which is the universe." That scenery, consisting of substandard schools, overpriced, dilapidated housing, poor medical care, unemployment, and a welfare system designed to degrade and divide, remains as a constant reminder that the universe will continue in its drabness, its poverty, and its brutality. If the universe will not yield, then it is the individual who must succumb and somehow try to accommodate himself to a limited and static existence.

The process of accommodating oneself to a life essentially devoid of possibilities is not easy. It is not simple to learn to accept one's impotence in a world supposedly replete with surging energy and ever-increasing mastery. Constant reminders of what might have been intrude themselves into the squalor that surrounds and imprisons one's consciousness. And so, the job of managing one's own misery is fraught with difficulty; it requires an enormous expenditure of energy, the kind of psychological energy which, when coupled with the physical and spiritual debilitation that invariably accompanies the loss of hope, eventually leads to the development of emotional instability. Symptoms abound as the individual's life stress increases (Langner & Michaels, 1963; Dohrenwend, 1967). Anxiety, depression, hostility, fear, withdrawal, and depersonalization begin to wreak havoc on the person already besieged with the problem of adapting himself to an encapsulated existence. Consequently, as indicated below (see Figure 3), the process of accommodation does not run smoothly.

The individual thrashes about, alternately lashing out, striving anew, and falling back in despair. He is in dire need of help in order to restore a semblance of stability to a life increasingly viewed as disrupted, irresponsible, and self-defeating.

By and large, the help that is forthcoming, traditionally provided by the mental health professions to people dealing with real-life problems, has tended to focus attention on the

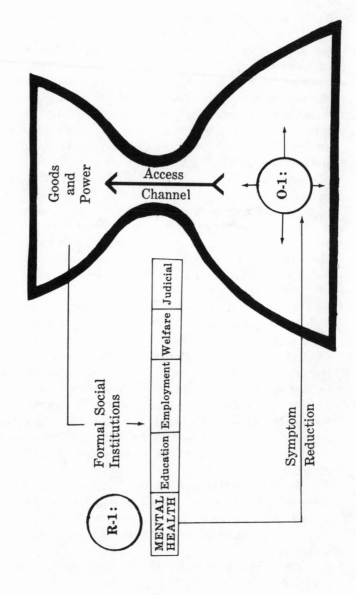

Figure 3. Option 1-Response 1: Adjustment

74

intrapsychic barriers to healthy adaptation. The treatment seeks to reduce or eliminate symptoms of depression, anxiety, and so on, which interfere with adjustment or emerge as a by-product of the process (Adams & McDonald, 1968; de Chenne, 1973). There is little evidence to suggest the validity or even the appropriateness of such psychotherapeutically oriented interventions (Rae-Grant, Gladwin & Bower, 1965; Goldenberg, 1973). The purpose of the treatment, however, is clear: to in some way help the individual adjust to his or her plight with a modicum of real or imagined dignity.[6] The cry for assistance meets with a response from the social institution charged with the task of protecting and promoting the mental health of citizens. And that response generally involves encouraging and facilitating the beleaguered individual's adjustment to a society that has systematically deceived and destroyed him.

Option 2-Response 2:
In Search and Support of Tokens

As previously indicated (see section entitled *America II*), it would be unwise to underestimate the lengths to which a basically inequitable social order will go to create the illusion of its essential "openness." Thus, for example, we have already reviewed the enormous effort that is expended in disseminating the goods and power message equally to all citizens. It is an effort which involves considerable resources, requires a good deal of time, and must, if it is to achieve its long-range social objectives, result in the "emancipation" of sufficient numbers of individuals to justify the enterprise. It is in this context that it becomes important for us to examine what we have called the "search and support of tokens."

A token is usually thought of as a symbol or sign which gives the semblance of genuineness. In terms of the existing social order, the concept is used to describe those individuals belonging to a generally excluded class who are found in positions usually denied to other members of their group. More often than not, the positions in question have a degree of public visibility, command a certain amount of respect and responsibility, and the selected individuals occupying those positions are perceived as serving the system by being available for being trotted out whenever their visibility can be used as proof of the system's inherent good faith.

Unfortunately, the prevailing definition of a token is very restrictive. It focuses attention on the very few individuals who are granted a disproportionate amount of apparent leverage by the system. It immediately conjures up images of Supreme Court Justices (Felix Frankfurter and Thurgood Marshall), United States Senators (Edward Brooke, Margaret Chase Smith, and Abraham Ribicoff), and others (Reverend Leon Sullivan, Ralph Bunche, and Barbara Walters) in positions to achieve broad public exposure. Moreover, in some vague manner it envelops its individuals in an amorphous cloak of heroism to reinforce the notion that courage, hard work, and determination are sufficient tools for rising significantly above one's original station in life. What the usual conception of a token does not do, however, is convey the system's need for such individuals at much lower levels in the social order, at levels of aspiration more easily identified with by the remaining masses of disenfranchised individuals. Its obvious showcase tokens aside, the system needs relatively large numbers of people to occupy positions in professional, middle-management, skilled craftsmen, and academic categories, for example, which are socially and economically removed but psychologically proximal to the oppressed groups from which the position holders come. As indicated below (see Figure 4), it is important that the system recruit, prepare, and process through its access channel sufficient numbers of its traditionally exploited citizens to perpetuate the myth of the system's unqualified responsiveness to all. The job of searching for and supporting these less publicized, less powerful but ultimately more instrumental, tokens rests with the formal social institutions, primarily those settings which are defined as helping in nature. At this point, a personal example might be instructive of the process.

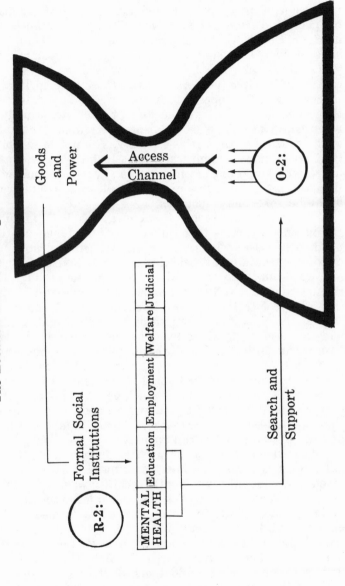

Figure 4. Option 2-Response 2:
The Location and Processing of Tokens

77

It is with a certain roguish pride that I now look back upon some of my early educational experiences. Like many of my peers and friends, I conceived of the public schools much as Henri Charriere, the central character in *Papillon*, must have viewed the island to which he was condemned: school was a place from which to escape, regardless of the time, cost, or effort involved. And during those rare spells when escape was truly impossible, school was to be treated with that same mixture of fear, contempt, and awe usually reserved for missionaries hell-bent on "civilizing the native" at the expense of the native's civility. The public school was the first of many amphitheaters in which the individual and his society would meet in hand-to-hand combat. And, as was the case in the coliseums of old, the ultimate result was usually a foregone conclusion.

The particular school I attended was indistinguishable from so many others that reigned over the tenement-filled neighborhoods in which they were located. A drab, nondescript building, it held its captives in a vise of concrete and wood where teachers who had long since relinquished their dreams dutifully went about the business of shaping the reality of children whose ill-fitting clothes and oily, stinking lunch bags were anything but inspiring. Oh, if they had only been assigned to teach in some school in the West Bronx or even Parkchester where "there was something to work with." But here they were in the East Bronx, among Emma Lazarus' "wretched masses," condemned to a building whose walls were continually cracking and children whose parents couldn't speak English and probably didn't care to. Fate had indeed dealt the teachers a cruel hand—and many of them played it out with a vengeance.

I recall very little about my first few years in school. In part, of course, this is because I was there so rarely. On any given day, particularly when the weather wasn't too bad, I, along with a couple of my friends, would leave the house with no intention of going to school. Instead, we'd meet in the alley behind Shechter's candy store, pick up a few other stray truants, and take off for places to be decided on in ways too numerous and convoluted to describe. Sometimes we'd wind up at the trolley barns on Southern Boulevard, lunge onto the backs of the outgoing cars, and ride the trolleys around the

Bronx. Other days would see us loping through the vacant lots and alleyways that connected the tenements, or leaping from one roof to another in awkward games of "Chicken." At other times, especially when it was warm, we'd either lounge on the hot, oozing, tarred roofs of our neighborhood and tell lies or camp on the third-floor fire escape of my building hoping against hope that we'd catch a glimpse of Big Gloria Milonas and one of her customers. But most of the time we'd just hang around, satisfied in the knowledge that "doing nothing" was eminently better than being in a place where Mrs. Hawkins' distaste for our ancestry was clear, where Mr. Klein's penchant for punishing transgressors ran the gamut from simple smacks in the mouth to more inventive tortures like making us stand on the narrow blackboard ledge which held the chalk and erasers and grasp the top of the blackboard's wooden frame while he belted us on the back with a ruler, or where Miss Tuttleman shared with us, ever so gently, her special knowledge that God's love for us was everlasting even though we had "killed Christ and wouldn't amount to anything."

One particularly predictable aspect of my early education was the knowledge that my mother would be summoned to school at least twice each semester. These summonses always signified trouble. To begin with, if they occurred at a time when my mother was working, it meant the loss of at least half a day's pay—a situation guaranteed to upset her regardless of the reason behind the school's "invitation." Also, it meant that she would have to be with people with whom she felt self-conscious, in a setting where she felt and was made to feel both uncomfortable and incompetent. But, most importantly, it meant being subjected to another hour-long review of the catalog of horrors that was her son.

An unchanging script dominated each of these parent-teacher conferences. First, there was the commiseration phase of the meeting. "We know you're a good, hard working woman Mrs. Goldenberg, and we hate to always be giving you bad news, Mrs. Goldenberg, but what can we do, Mrs. Goldenberg, he's your son, not ours, Mrs. Goldenberg, and each of us must bear our own cross as best we can, Mrs. Goldenberg." Next came the indictment. "He plays hookey; he's always fighting; he won't do his work; he's insolent; curses all the time, can't sit still, and, oh well, you know, Mrs. Goldenberg, you're his poor mother." Then came the diagnosis. "Mrs. Goldenberg, we both know there's something terribly wrong with him. Maybe he's a little retarded, you know, slow, maybe mentally disturbed, a little crazy, or something." And finally, the prescription. "Maybe, if we all work enough, Mrs. Goldenberg, we can get him into a trade school someday; who knows what can happen with someone like him? Maybe with more discipline in the home . . . why not talk with your social worker some more, Mrs. Goldenberg? . . . Lots can be done these days with slow and disturbed kids."

My mother would sit, head bowed, nodding occasionally in assent, clasping and unclasping her fingers, a stony picture of dejection, despair, and failure. When it was finally all over and she was shuffling out of the office, she'd look at me and we'd both know there were uneasy and angry days ahead. There would be some harsh words, maybe a licking, a few new promises, a few old threats, but nothing that couldn't be managed or eventually undone.

And so it went. Four times each school year the curtain would rise, the short, four-act drama would be played out, the curtain would fall, and the players would once again retire to their respective dressing rooms to await and agonize over the expected reviews. Life was predictable, or at least we thought so—until around 1945.

The ending of World War II ushered in a new era of testing in the public schools. Buoyed perhaps by the success of diagnostic testing in the armed forces, or simply because of the need to reabsorb large numbers into an increasingly shaky peacetime economy, a vast intelligence testing program was mounted in the elementary schools. The diagnosticians descended like a host of locusts eating their way across some previously virgin terrain. Few schools escaped their embrace and almost no students were spared the experience of being lined up, ushered into large rooms or gymnasiums, and undergoing the testing ritual. The teachers loved it. For at least a couple of days they wouldn't have to face their thirty-odd charges in direct and lonely

confrontation. Even the kids liked it. It was a brief change in
routine, something different, even noisy for a little
while—Christmas come early.

As fate would have it, I happened to be in school on the
day the locusts hit P.S. 61. Some of my friends, of course,
weren't. But I, like the rest of my classmates, dutifully went
through the period of processing which included taking that
variety of tests, "games," and other assorted activities
covered by the term "assessment." And, while to this day I
cannot recall any of the specifics of the tests I took, I am
absolutely convinced that my future was guaranteed during
that day in 1945 in the musky gymnasium of P.S. 61.

About three or four weeks after the tests were
administered my mother was summoned to school. I was a bit
startled by this, not because my behavior had changed—I
was still playing hookey, getting into fights, and generally
going about my business as usual—but because it was only
October and my mother's first summoning rarely occurred
before the middle of November. At any rate, my mother
showed up at the appointed time and appeared fully steeled
for the expected rerun of the well-rehearsed drama entitled
"Poor Mrs. Goldenberg."

But no sooner had the curtain gone up than it appeared
that a new play had come to town. Someone had thrown out
the old script and had substituted a new one. Smiles
abounded as my mother was now informed of the vast
"potential" she had so painfully ejected from her womb some
nine years before. She was given her son's IQ score, a number
which, while much lower than her own Social Security
number, was supposedly cause for instant rejoicing. We
looked at each other, wondering if perhaps we had wandered
into the wrong theater. As the new plot continued to unfold,
it became clear that I was no longer the dumb or disturbed
child that the school had always maintained I was. All of a
sudden my previous behavior had nothing to do with any
genetic defect or developmental flaw in my character. Indeed,
as we now came to find out, my playing hookey, fighting,
insolence—in short, all those things that had led to my being
viewed as incorrigible—were little more than simple and
"understandable responses" to "not being intellectually

challenged or properly stimulated." Voila! The toad had been transformed into a prince, his ugliness made beautiful by a magic number.

From that day on my life, particularly the part of it connected with school, changed significantly. I became nothing less than a "project," the object of such individual and group ministrations as to shame most current efforts at compensatory education. Tutors, remedial education folk of all types and persuasions, and specialized instructors flitted about me like so many bees hovering around some particularly exotic flower suddenly discovered to be growing in a vacant city lot. Escape became increasingly difficult, and playing hookey almost impossible. No sooner would I leave the house, indeed open the apartment door, than I would literally run into my teacher or some other emissary from the school patiently waiting for me in the bleak hallway. How long had they been standing there? Neither snow, nor rain, nor dark of night kept them from their appointed round. And in the school it was the same. No longer could I hide, avoid, or in any other manner undermine my "educational development." Help, whether requested or not, fell upon me like a sudden summer cloud burst. I was drenched in remedial experiences of every kind and description. Older children were assigned to break through the fortress I had erected to learning long division; my ability to read became a group project involving several teachers and tutors, all hell-bent on guaranteeing my mastery of *Treasure Island*; accompanied weekly trips to the public library became a permanent part of my educational fare; and counseling—oh, the endless one-to-one counseling —for anything and everything. It was, in short, a situation in which my ultimate ability to benefit from the educational experience was as unquestioned as the previous belief that I would never, under any circumstances, "amount to anything." My future, and those of a few other residents of P.S. 61, was "guaranteed" in the autumn of 1945. The months and years that were to follow would, of course, bring with them their own brand of problems and anxieties. But they would be the problems of making it, not the repeated agonies of constantly unfulfilled hope.

The point, of course, of this perhaps overly long personal vignette is not to denigrate the efforts of those who tried to help me. The real issue is one that transcends individuals and is independent of individual outcomes, for it revolves around the fundamental question of "real" as opposed to artificially and temporarily created access in a social system which for all intents and purposes remains essentially closed (Coles, 1969). The "relish," as Paros (1973) puts it, with which I was treated subsequent to undergoing the testing ritual only becomes significant in the light of those who, either because their "magic number" was not as high as mine or because they were absent at the time of testing, *did not* receive the attention and help accorded me. It is from this perspective that we must view the question of special help or compensatory education, and it is from this perspective that we must judge the underlying motivations and goals of the formal social institutions involved in the search and support of tokens.

Option 3-Response 3:
Criminality and the Control of Deviance

There is, of course, a third option available to those who eventually come to realize that their efforts will never result in penetrating the supposedly nonexistent barrier that separates them from the system's publicized earthly rewards. That option, such as it is, involves *striking out, and trying to break through* the walls which limit the conditions under which one is forced to live. More often than not, such actions result in what is called "criminal" or "deviant" behavior, but in terms of our current analysis it is important that we try to understand such behavior in the context of what we have called the "American experience." More precisely, there are at least two ways in which such behavior can be interpreted, and both interpretations necessitate a concurrent analysis of the increasing role of the helping professions in the criminal justice system.

For many of the traditionally discarded, particularly those who cannot adjust or be adjusted to having comparatively little and those not fortunate enough to become a part of the singling-out process that produces mini-tokens, the essential ungivingness of the system comes into direct conflict with the taking ethos that underlies the system's omnipresent goods and power message. Barred from acquiring goods and power through legitimate means, yet dominated by the unchallenged persuasiveness of the message, some choose to extract goods and power through means which are either illegal or antisocial. The ensuing criminality can be viewed as behavior which affirms the prevailing social ethos, albeit via routes which are not socially confirming. Criminal behavior is "taking behavior," and in that sense it is consistent with the exploitative and competitive orientations under which the broader society functions. The fact that such behavior is generally class confined, that is, usually carried out by members of a particular socioeconomic class on others of that class, should, of course, not be overlooked, for it highlights both the efficacy with which the goods and power message has been disseminated as well as the seductiveness of its appeal (Reckless, 1950; Sutherland & Cressey, 1955). As Cole (1970) puts it: "Violent, self-destructive, and antisocial actions are an attempt to come to grips with the lack of power, because no one willingly accepts imposed impotence. Especially not in a society that makes such a fetish of power."

A second and comparatively more recent interpretation of what are usually termed criminal or deviant acts revolves around the view that such behaviors are either implicitly or explicitly political in either focus or nature. Thus, when Cleaver (1968) writes that the only way black people know of making withdrawals from the bank is "at the point of a gun," he is dealing as much with the political symbolism of oppression as with the definition of armed robbery. Similarly, when Aptheker (1971) and Marcuse (1970) analyze the uses to which such concepts as "law and order" are put, they are describing a situation in which both the antecedents and the consequences of the criminal act become interpretable within a particular revolutionary perspective. It is, in short, the kind of perspective which rejects the notion of alleged criminal characteristics residing within the individual and, instead, projects the deviant or criminal act onto the much larger screen of society itself. Such a projection can only result when the concept of criminality becomes an integral part of a far more fundamental analysis of the contradictions that define a social order's basic purpose and processes.

In any event, it is clear that most antisocial or criminal acts result in behaviors which are both figuratively and literally confrontal, in which the actor strikes out against an existing social norm or institution. This fact alone guarantees the involvement, not only of the traditional law enforcement agencies and their judicial counterparts, but also of the formal social institution, the helping professions, charged with the problems of defining and controlling deviant behavior.

There is little doubt that the mental health professions are becoming increasingly involved in the prevention of crime and more importantly in the treatment of adjudicated offenders (Steiner, 1973). This involvement takes many forms and covers such dimensions as the basic interpretation of criminality, specific program planning, the training of personnel, and the rehabilitation of those already incarcerated (Goldenberg, 1973; McArthur, 1973; Reppucci et. al., 1973; Katkin & Sibley, 1973).[7] Certainly, the criminal justice system is currently in a state of flux, with movements often occurring simultaneously in such diverse and seemingly mutually exclusive areas as deinstitutionalization on the one hand and the utilization of neurosurgical, behavior modification, and psychopharmacological techniques to control and change behavior on the other.

By and large, however (see Figure 5), the increased involvement of the helping professions in the problems associated with crime has not changed the traditional orientation and role of the mental health professional in the criminal justice system. That role has revolved around the functions

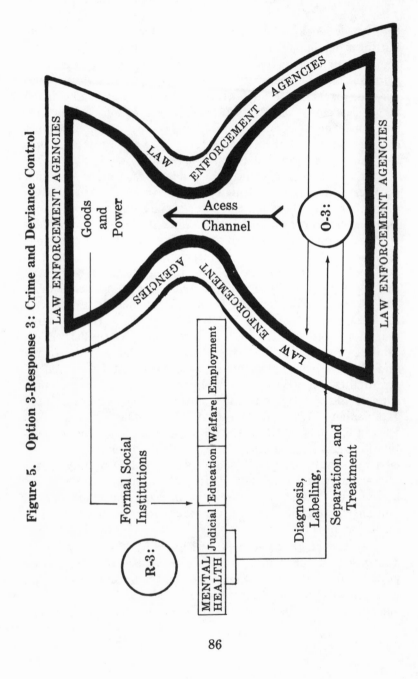

Figure 5. Option 3-Response 3: Crime and Deviance Control

86

associated with diagnosing, labeling, separating, and perhaps treating the offender. Whether the mental health professional is involved at an early stage in the adjudication process, as is more and more the case with respect to the youthful offender, or relatively late in the game, at or long after institutionalization has taken place, his basic orientation has been to reinforce the premise of individual pathology. As such, his input and skills have been focused on the problems of deviance control, his ultimate impact relegated to issues of systems maintenance, not questions of individual and group liberation.

Option 4-Response 4:
Involuntary Alienation and the Saving of Souls

There is, of course, one final option, not counting suicide but psychologically analogous to it, available to the individual who finally perceives the basic futility of his position. It is an option that can be called "involuntary alienation," for it involves the individual exempting himself from the social order, generally via the process of chemical dissociation, that is, through the reliance on drugs or alcohol as the principal way of insulating oneself against the unending meaninglessness of a barren existence.

More often than not, the term "alienation" is used to describe a state of being characterized by a pervasive sense of psychological estrangement from the world of which one remains a physical part. In its most extreme form it manifests itself as a spiritual disengagement which is so profound as to render the individual totally disconnected from the experiential climate in which he is nominally embedded. The alienated individual removes himself from others, continually wandering the endless subterranean caverns that encircle the body politic. His only mission is to seek oblivion or momentarily heightened consciousness through which his own existence becomes bearable.

For the person who is either too incorrigible to be adjusted, not fortunate enough to be selected out, or too smart or frightened to become a full-time criminal, the only option available through which the reality of never making it within the system can be dealt with is the one we have termed *involuntary alienation through chemical dissociation*. Before proceeding any further, it is important to define the concept more clearly. To begin with, let us understand that involuntary alienation is not a true option in the traditional sense, that is, it is not an alternative choice which brings with it the possibilities of any substantial improvement in the existential condition. It is, instead, a preference for how one's own meaninglessness will be defined. In addition, we call it involuntary to further convey the notion that the circumstances which lead an individual to choose this so-called option are not substantially under the individual's control. It is not, for example, the kind of alienation which, if tried and found to be unsatisfying, can easily be transformed into another mode of being. That form of alienation, voluntary alienation, has been described by Keniston (1965) and Reich (1970) and is a rather luxurious form of disengagement available to those of relative affluence and, of course, their usually highly educated children.[8] Finally, the kind of involuntary alienation described usually depends on drugs or alcohol to reach the level of dissociation required to attain temporary relief. Here again, even the kinds of drugs used by those who are rendered involuntarily alienated differs from the pattern of drug use characteristic among those who freely choose to become alienated. For example, the drugs traditionally used by poor people have been of the hard variety, drugs which, in effect, serve to turn off the environment and temporarily stop the endless bombardment of the senses by external stimuli. In contrast, at least until very recently, the drugs taken by those we have called voluntarily alienated, the "seekers" from backgrounds of plenty, have tended to be of the mind-expanding variety, such as the psychedelics, which act to enhance and intensify sensory experiences (Goldenberg, et. al., 1972).

In Figure 6 we have depicted the "option" of involuntary

Figure 6. Option 4-Response 4: Involuntary Alienation and the Saving of Souls

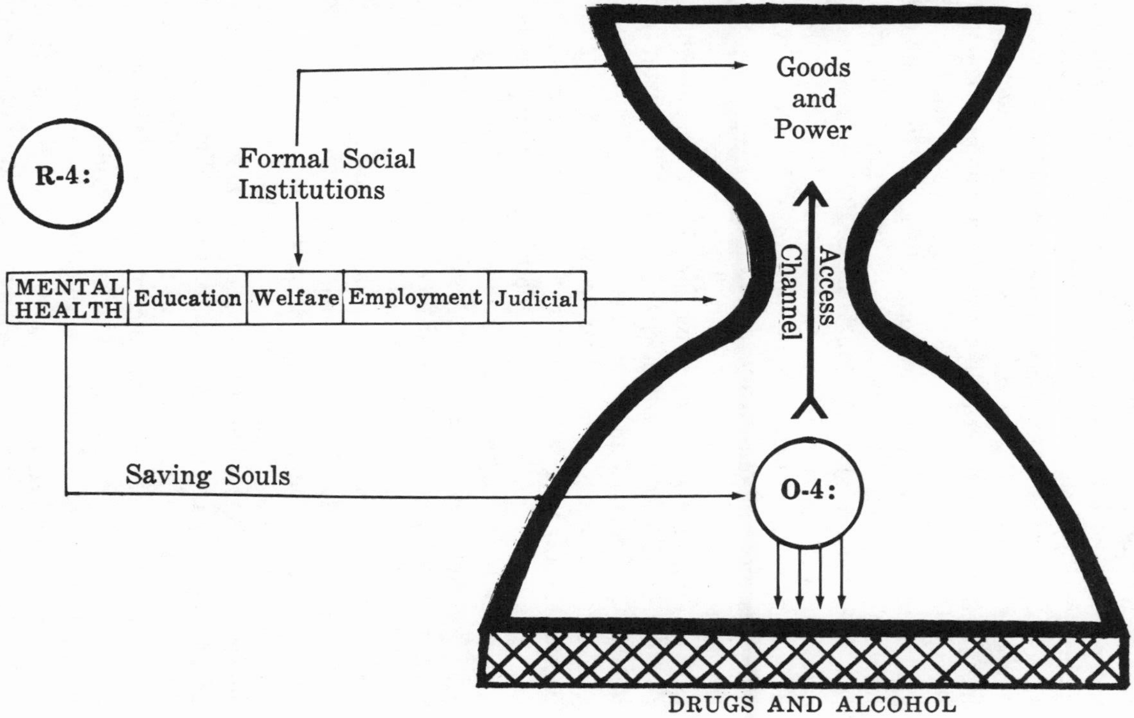

Goods
and
Power

Access
Channel

O-4:

DRUGS AND ALCOHOL

Formal Social
Institutions

MENTAL HEALTH | Education | Welfare | Employment | Judicial

Saving Souls

R-4:

alienation as it applies to those who eventually choose it as a way of dealing with the prevailing social order and their own nonviability with respect to that social order. In addition, we have illustrated the response of the helping professions to such people, a response we shall call the *saving of souls*.

In explaining Figure 6, we would ask the reader to imagine a grid, screen, or gratelike structure which extends along the entire bottom portion of the imperfect hourglass. This grid keeps people in the system, albeit as "untroublesome failures" (Option 1: ◄┤►), "selected tokens" (Option 2: ▲▲ ▲▲), or "criminals" (Option 3: ✖ ✖). Those, however, who cannot or will not remain a part of the social order, those who do not settle into the available slots, are the people who finally become involuntarily alienated and eventually fall through the openings in the grid. They descend to a level of personal oblivion in which drugs or alcohol become the only anchors of solace. For them, even though the presumed validity of the goods and power message may remain a fixed and unquestioned part of their consciousness, the total impact of the experience of recurrent failure becomes the critical variable accounting for their descent. They are the people who come to inhabit the netherworld of domestic exiles.

For the mental health professional, the domestic exile represents a psychological syndrome of such profound pathology and seriousness as to warrant intervention aimed at the immediate retrieval of the individual from the depths to which he has fallen. The acknowledged anomic existence of the drug addict and the chronic alcoholic, especially when coupled with the currently explosive nature of the rhetoric surrounding their alleged behaviors, has elevated the addict and alcoholic, particularly the hard-core addict, from a position of mild social revulsion to one of "constituting a national problem." Amid statements concerning their negative impact on the economy, not to mention their responsibility for the increase in street crime, those who have fallen through the grid have assumed a status rarely accorded to involuntary subterraneans in our culture (Wilkor & Rasor, 1953; Kurtis,

1970; Stewart, 1970). Not surprisingly, the mental health professions constitute an important regiment in the new army being assembled to wage war on the problems of addicton, that is, on those who are addicted. What is the basic response of the helping professions to the involuntarily alienated? It is not, of course, one which seeks to examine and change the institutional forces at the heart of the drug problem. Such a response would be inimical to the nature of formal social institutions of which the mental health establishment is an integral part. Rather, the response, often couched in the most humane and lofty of terms, is to "save" the addict, to rescue him from himself and the abyss into which he has fallen. It is an almost religious response, one steeped in the endless possibilities of human redemption. But, as is the case with respect to the issue of causation, questions concerning the purpose of this redemption remain either unasked or unanswered. Factually, there is no evidence to indicate that supposedly saving the addict will result in any basic change in the objective conditions of his life. The inability to grant him greater access to the system's rewards does not materially affect the zeal with which the mental health professional pursues its quarry. As was the case in the crusades of old, fervor replaces meaning, and the saving of souls is its own reward.

America IV: The Flip Side of the Coin

This chapter has been concerned primarily with the problem of conceptualizing the American experience in terms of its consequences for the traditionally and historically oppressed and those most directly and obviously excluded from participating viably in the social order. However, since the ultimate purpose of our analysis is to create a framework for understanding the possibilities and limits of social intervention, it is necessary to spend some time looking at the "flip side of the coin," at the conditions confronting those who make it in the system, particularly those at levels which yield greater amounts of material goods without proportionate increases in real power.[9] Such an analysis, however brief, will highlight some of the problems of viewing the process of social intervention as either implying or requiring immediate intergroup cooperation (see Chapter 4).

Making it in our society is not without its problems, for, although having made it implies having acquired a greater share of the available goods and power, it does not follow that the person, simply because he need no longer deal with the question of survival on a daily basis, or because he now possesses greater control over his destiny, necessarily experiences the relief one would imagine to be consistent with this elevated status. This is particularly true of those we call middle class, those who have meandered through the access channel and now reside somewhere "in the middle" of that portion of the hourglass from which the goods and power flow. If success brings with it certain survival guarantees, it does not immunize the individual from experiencing the contradictions which encapsulate his existence. What success often does is liberate the individual to deal with questions of the quality of life rather than questions of survival. Issues of "existential meaning" and "transcendence" become relevant primarily when questions of basic survival have receded into the background. Nevertheless, such issues are real, and, while they may appear to be luxuries to those who must forever grapple to get mind and body through each day, they are, certainly from a social interventionist's point of view, potentially important.

Much has been written about the problems of making it in a superindustrialized society (Riesman, Glazer & Denny, 1950; Stein, Vidich & White, 1960). Philosophers (Buber, 1956; Camus, 1959), educators (Goodman, 1956; Lerner, 1962), and social scientists (May, 1960; Slater & Bennis, 1968) alike have provided endless tales and descriptions of the anxiety and quiet desperation that mark the lives of middle-class people in contemporary society. Such ills as the seemingly interminable identity crisis and the ever-present loss of the sense of self appear to be almost endemic in that part of the population which is perceived as both economically and socially substantial. The picture created is that of a life which for all its material solvency remains emotionally and interpersonally bankrupt.

For the purposes of the analysis being developed in this chapter, it is interesting to review the responses of the helping professions to the problems presented by those who have supposedly made it within the framework of the existing social order. Some fascinating parallels emerge when comparing these responses with the actions generally taken toward the masses of the poor and totally powerless. Some differences also emerge, but here too the nature of the differences is more than a little instructive.

Since, as we have indicated, making it or, more accurately, having made it brings its own brand of problems, it stands to reason that the individual so affected must develop specific ways of dealing with whatever pain or discomfort he is experiencing. These options often turn out to resemble, at least in broad form, those employed by many of their disenfranchised counterparts. In addition, the responses of the helping professions to the particular options chosen by those experiencing "dis-ease" are not discernibly different, especially with respect to basic intent, from the ones employed with the traditionally oppressed. For example, in Figures 7, 8, and 9 we have depicted both the behavioral options available to "enfranchised sufferers" as well as responses made to their suffering by members of the formal social institution, the mental health establishment, charged with defining, detecting, and controlling deviance.

Figure 7 describes the situation that confronts those members of the middle classes who, after attaining some goods and power, cannot avoid reflecting upon the price that was extracted from them as a condition or consequence of becoming deeply involved in the process of acquiring. Think, for example, of the middle-level corporate executive whose life of "liquid lunches," meaningless meetings, and endless organizational backbitings leaves in its wake an emptiness of

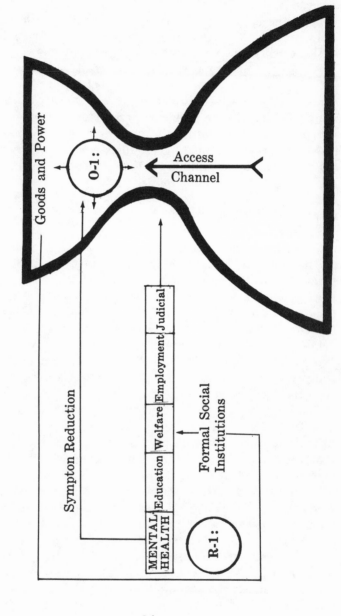

Figure 7: Option 1-Response 1: Adjustment

Goods and Power

O-1:

Access Channel

Sympton Reduction

MENTAL HEALTH | Education | Welfare | Employment | Judicial

Formal Social Institutions

R-1:

94

Figure 8. Option 2-Response 2: Open Revolt and Deviance Control

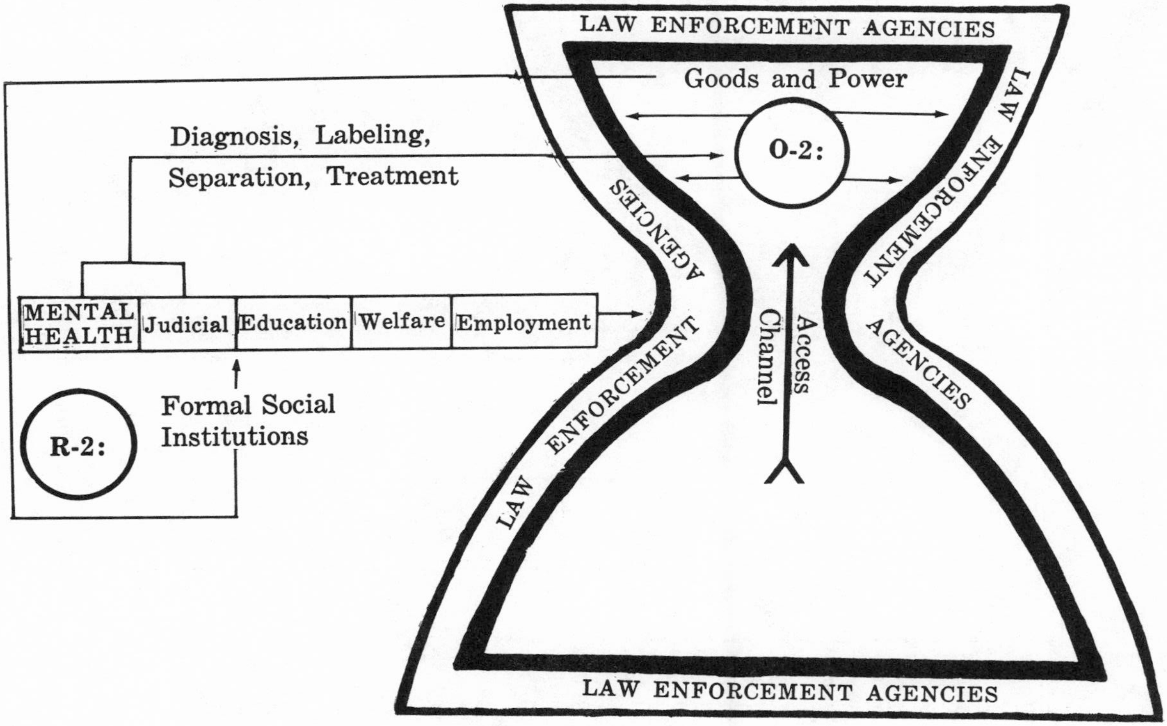

95

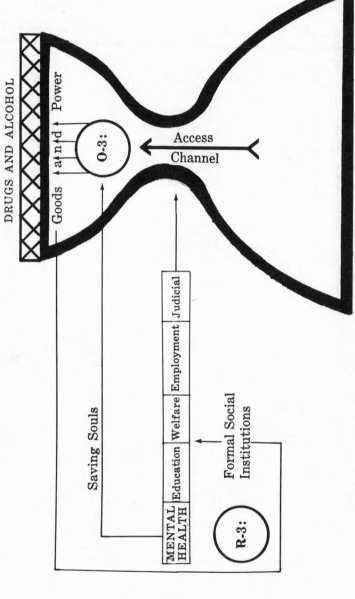

Figure 9. Option 3-Response 3: Voluntary Alienation and Imposed Salvation

purpose which signifies little more than wasted years and misspent energies. Or the successful salesman whose prowess depends on the ability to cultivate an ever-changing artificial personality which gradually comes to replace that which was once real and vital. Or, perhaps most obviously, the suburban housewife for whom the emptiness of the tract mentality becomes a gnawing and constant reminder of an unlived life of endless dependency and reflected status. In each case, we find individuals whose suffering is as much a part of the process by which goods and power are acquired as was the suffering of those for whom the acquisition of such goods and power is next to impossible. Again, the traditional response of the helping professions to this expressed pain takes the form of symptom reduction. When confronted with the sufferer, albeit now the middle-class sufferer, the mental health professional, rather than dealing with the systemic bases of the pain, tends to focus his attention and that of the clients' on the possibilities of adjusting to instead of changing the objective situation.

His interventions, whether they focus attention on trying to work through personal anxiety, develop hobbies to alleviate tension, or form outside interests to reduce depression, are likely to be oriented toward the dual problems of individual adaptation and maintenance of the system. Similarly, when it comes to dealing with those who develop antisocial behaviors as a way of expressing the contradictions they recognize in their lives, the least common denominator of responses, that is, diagnosing, labeling, separating, and treating, again emerges as the prepotent one (Figure 8). Thus, whether dealing with white collar crime or the increasing tendency of affluent white youth to engage in acts of "revolutionary violence," the tendency is to treat such behaviors as individual aberrations, as instances of profound and exotic pathology.

Finally, there are those who, after having feasted on the goods and power that constitute the system's preferred menu, leave the table feeling strangely empty, still hungry, their appetites not sated by the morsels already consumed (Figure 9). For these people, primarily the children of the affluent, an altered consciousness develops which sees the loss of intimacy, openness, and spontaneity as too high a price to pay for the plastic and tenuous security being offered to them. For them the pursuit of goods and power becomes synonymous with dehumanization and artificiality. Having tasted of the system's fruits and having found them wanting, they voluntarily reject the cultural imperative and choose instead to pursue alternative life-styles and "better" ways of relating to an increasingly romanticized universe. Living things, the earth, the senses, and an as-yet undefined but purposefully apolitical spirituality become the heart of movement, the fulcrum for a new kind of "seeking." Often the search leads to drugs, alcohol, or other forms of mind-expanding and consciousness-raising activities. They may become runaways, street people, or members of communities committed to primitivizing life in ways presumed to be more consistent with the "natural order of things." But, regardless of what they do, their behavior symbolizes a conscious volitional rejection of the values underlying their socialization. They voluntarily opt out of the system through an imaginary grate, this time at the top, rather than the bottom, of the imperfect hourglass.[10] Here again, as was the case with respect to the poor who leave the system, the act of opting out, since it often involves drugs, alcohol, or results in deviant patterns of living, attracts the attention of the helping professions. Once more there are souls to be saved, individuals to be reclaimed. To be sure, the approach of the mental health worker to the voluntarily alienated is significantly more studied and sophisticated than is the case with respect to the hard-core domestic exile. After all, it is, at least symbolically, his own children that are now involved. But be this as it may, and granting the increased personal concern, the basic approach is still one which treats the problem of alienation as symptomatic of some kind of disordered or peculiarly idiosyncratic response to the acknowledged stresses and strains of growing up. Time and patience will ultimately prevail, but in the meantime imposed salvation is not without its own rewards.

In this chapter we have developed a framework for understanding what we have called the "American experience." It is a framework within which the problems of oppression emerge not as instances of individual or unprogramed cruelty, but as predictable patterns of exclusion whose roots are firmly embedded in the assumptive bases of the social order. By focusing on the inevitable consequences of a goods and power ideology, we have traced the routes by which the oppressive theme both acquires its surface validity and insures its survival. The primary purpose of this analysis, however, was to create the conceptual ground out of which attempts at social intervention emerge. Consequently, it is to the problems, prospects, and practice of social intervention that we now turn.

4

The Problems, Prospects, and Practice of Social Intervention

The practice of social intervention is serious and difficult and the criteria for success are forever fluid and changing and sometimes elusive. Perhaps that is as it must be, for whether or not change occurs often depends on miniscule, almost imperceptible alterations in the complex equation governing the manner in which people are controlled. The forces against change are formidable. They include not only the well-known and oft-reviled "vested interests," but also the entire cultural mosaic within which the "American experience" is defined and played out (see Chapter 3). This experience, so rich in its contradictions, so tormented by its legacies, so fortified, legitimized, and rationalized over time, is as disabling and intimidating as any array of easily identifiable institutional constraints. While it may be no more than a glimpse of the obvious, it would be fair to say that in attempting to effect some meaningful change in the conditions under which people live, the social interventionist is confronted, though in microscopic form, with the entire panorama of social history. He intervenes at a time and place long since removed from the actual onset of the problem. His first and only lasting allies are the pain he must terminate and the anger or despair with which he must contend.

The purpose of this chapter is *not* to provide a blueprint and set of tactics for social action. The reader primarily interested in reviewing existing intervention strategies would do well to look elsewhere. Alinsky (1969, 1971), for example, has provided a wealth of material, both theorietical and practical, concerning the possibilities and pitfalls of social intervention. His analyses of mass organizing, leadership, and the tactics of conflict, crisis, and confrontation remain among the clearest statements yet of how to conduct the "business" of social change. The work of Ecklein and Lauffer (1972) provides valuable case studies in the general area of social intervention. Their examples, drawn from such diverse activities as rent strikes, neighborhood organizing, and social planning, are illustrative of the manner in which certain techniques can be used to apply pressure and, more generally, create the atmosphere in which change occurs. Brown's (1972) manual on store-front organizing is as concrete an example as can be found of the problems of developing local movements for purposes of influencing and directing events. Similarly, the works of Aronowitz (1964), Gans (1965), Dellinger (1965), Rustin (1966), Cloward and Elman (1968), Oppenheimer (1969), and Altshuler (1970) are useful in developing an understanding of the role of advocacy, "guerilla tactics," civil disobedience, and community control in the problems associated with change. Even Haley's (1969) essay on the power tactics of Jesus Christ provides some valuable insights into the strategies associated with the development of effective organizations. Finally, the writings of Harrington (1962), Marris and Rein (1967), and Coles (1968) offer acceptable analyses of the broader social, political, psychological, and economic frameworks within which specific attempts to effect change are embedded. There is, in short, no dearth of material, some more useful than others and some more real than others, on the specifc tactics and strategies that enter into social intervention.

Given the above, *the purpose of this chapter is to examine the functional context within which change agents operate,* to focus attention on what we believe to be some of the rarely discussed issues that ultimately influence both the course and direction of most efforts to alter living conditions. Our point of departure for this analysis is the definition and dimensions we already have developed for differentiating the social interventionist from the social technician, the traditional social reformer, and so on, who often masquerade in his garb (see Chapter 1). In other words, we start from a perspective in which the change agent is fundamentally at odds with the system's underlying assumptions and goals, perceives the need for basic institutional change, identifies himself directly with those whose oppression is most evident in the situation, and conceives of his task as involving the need to raise contradictions. He envisions his efforts, if successful, as resulting in an organizational strength and solidarity capable of significantly changing the existing balance of power without undue recourse to endless and potentially self-defeating violence. Furthermore, we start from a position predicated on the belief that an adherence to these precepts, even when coupled with a demonstrated command of the existing strategies and tactics of social intervention, may not prove effective unless accompanied by a correspondingly critical awareness of what we have called the "functional context" of the intervention. The *functional context consists of the unanalyzed forces and conflicting currents that characterize the social interventionist's ideas and behavior.*

The Problems

All attempts to change the human condition are bounded by goals and mediated by processes. In the final analysis, the success of any interventionist venture depends on the degree of fit between these goals and processes on the one hand, and the people whose lives will be most directly impacted by their realization or nonrealization on the other. To the extent that this fit is contrived, artificially induced, or otherwise imposed, whether by an apparent insider or by an outside agent, the prospects for success, short- or long-term, are unworthy of serious consideration. To the degree, however, that there is an experientially valid link between where people are, where they see themselves going, and the manner in which they see themselves covering the intervening ground, to that degree can we begin to gauge the efficacy of an intervention, independent of whether or not there is an isomorphic relationship between the amount of energy invested in the amount of return immediately visible. It is, after all, ultimately the *people,* their needs, their analyses, their experiences, and their efforts, who constitute the irreducible base from which all attempts at social intervention derive their initial impetus and subsequent meaning, and it is the failure to take this fact seriously that accounts for much of the self-imposed mischief that often undermines the process of social change.

The failure of social interventionists to fully understand the contextual fabric within which they wish to operate is due to a variety of factors. In each instance, however, the error manifests itself in faulty analysis and inappropriate action or, most likely, in both. In each instance the result is to further complicate an already difficult undertaking.

1. Different Strokes for Different Folks

It is one thing to have an overall conception of the social and historical forces which produce an oppressive system; it is quite another to translate that conception into a form of action that is consistent with the experiences of any particular group. In Chapter 3, we compared and contrasted what we called the involuntary alienation of the poor and powerless with the voluntary alienation of those occupying higher, more economically secure positions in the social order. In both instances we saw people driven to the point where their continued membership in the existing body politic became a psychological and physical impossibility; in both instances we saw people leaving the system, seeking alternatives or falling prey to the temporary relief offered by any one of the increasing number of available narcotics; in both instances we saw people either being pushed out or opting out of a system they had been socialized to revere. And yet, for all the presumed phenotypic similarities between them, it was always abundantly clear that there were different dynamics at work in each case: the alienation of the poor stemmed from not having any goods and power; the alienation of the affluent came about because of the spiritual trade-off demanded by the goods and power ethos itself. The reality that both the poor and the affluent share certain aspects of the oppressive experience should neither obscure nor be confused with the very real and fundamental differences in the nexus of each group's captivity. The failure to understand these differences, to force an artificial, almost romantic affinity between groups occupying very dissimilar positions in the economic order, is to deny reality and, consequently, to prematurely sacrifice the interventionist effort on the altar of a philosophical premise which, for all its seductive universalism, can only impede the process of social change.

From a social interventionist perspective, there are basically only two ways to change conditions in a goods and power oriented society characterized by an underdeveloped class consciousness: *those who suffer from the absence of goods and power must be helped to acquire their fair share of the available resources, and those whose pain is a result of the endless psychological paying of dues demanded as the price for relative economic stability must be helped to develop alternative modes of relating to a superindustrialized technocracy.* In other words, the focus and definition of any social intervention must follow from, not precede, the experience of the particular socioeconomic group involved. For the traditionally excluded, social intervention means the wrenching from existing institutional sources of the goods and powers historically denied them; for the more affluent, it means the critical examination of those socially conditioned values which are at the heart of their growing emptiness. To assume, at least in this country and at this time, that groups occupying different positions in the economic system can easily transcend their own class interests, quickly form viable coalitions, and, together, begin to address themselves to the big questions is to indulge in a form of self-deception which bespeaks a marked underestimation of the meaning and power of the "American experience." This does not mean, of course, that interclass or intergroup cooperation is impossible, for, as we shall indicate, there are a number of different ways in which apparently dissimilar groups can identify the common sources of their oppression. Rather, it is meant to underscore both the importance of a class-specific orientation toward social intervention and the dangers of an overly romanticized view, the 1960s view, of the possibilities and pitfalls of significant intergroup collaboration.[1]

Outlined below (see Figure 1) are some of the more obvious consequences of a class-specific analysis for the development of change-oriented goals and strategies. As can be seen, there are very real differences in the kinds of issues (i.e., in the pain) that each group brings with it to the situation. Consequently, there are markedly different group goals and different routes by which these goals can be most effectively realized. There are also communalities but, if they are to lead eventually to any viable form of intergroup cooperation, they must first be approached in the context of each group's own needs and goals. The willingness and ability of poor people and those of relative affluence to transcend their socially conditioned separation depends in large part on the degree to which the mediation of class-specific objectives lends credibility to the need for a more universal approach to the overall question of bondage.

For those who are poor and traditionally excluded from the body politic, the major issues associated with social inter-

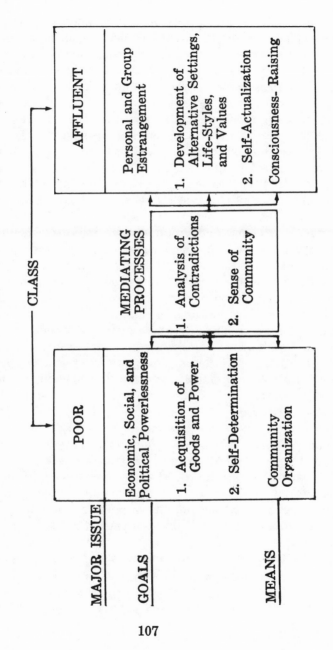

Figure 1. The Poor and the Affluent:
Social Intervention From a Class-Specific Orientation

vention initially rarely revolve around questions concerning the system's underlying philosophical validity. People who are struggling to survive and trying to deal with the cumulative effects of an imposed and debasing rhetoric concerning the presumed causes of their debilitation (e.g., the doctrine of personal culpability—see Chapter 1) should not be expected to approach their plight by focusing attention on the human condition in the abstract. For them social intervention is a bread and butter issue, an issue primarily defined in terms of how best and quickly to increase their economic, social, and political power. Thus, their goals center on the acquisition of items of goods and power which are both tangible and have come to symbolize the essence of their exclusion. Increased individual and group *self-determination* is the psychological referent in the struggle for resources. By self-determination is meant the ability to control the basic conditions under which survival takes place. The principal vehicle for the acquisition of goods and power as well as for the development of the self-determination that invariably accompanies the possession of greater economic and social resources lies in the dynamic of *community organization.* Community organization is the mechanism by which previously isolated and vulnerable individuals band together to identify and pursue common goals. For the poor, community organization is probably the most effective way of confronting an establishment whose power has to some degree always rested on its ability to keep oppressed people separated from one another, ever at each other's throats in the frantic quest for small individualized favors. As Alinsky once remarked: "Power just goes to two poles—to those who've got money, and those who've got people." Community organization is the means by which those who've really only got each other begin to realize that fact—and to act upon it.

For the affluent, on the other hand, the most significant existential issue to be dealt with revolves around the ever-increasing psychological estrangement that accompanies the successful pursuit of goods and power. The particular form of estrangement varies, but whether it manifests itself as a loss of self or in the now almost traditional departure, both physically and psychologically, of the young from the values and life-styles of their affluent parents, the feeling is one of an unaccountable aloneness and a sense of dull, pointless tragedy.[2] In either case, and our interest at this point is primarily focused on the adults, the need is for a rekindled sense of personal integrity, interpersonal closeness, and a sense of completeness that is more than symbolic in nature.[3] The goals of this group then, the experiential base with which the social interventionist must be able to identify, revolve around the development of alternative, nondebilitating ways of relating both to oneself and to the world. The goals, in short, are to reexamine the fundamental premises surrounding one's existence and the consequences of those premises on the manner in which one's life has become artificially compartmentalized. For purposes of description, these goals may be viewed as *self-actualizing* in intent, for they almost invariably deal with issues of intimacy, spontaneity, and the full flowering of one's creative potential. This being the case, the most appropriate vehicle to be used in the rekindling process is that of *consciousness-raising*. By consciousness-raising we mean the process by which people are confronted and forced to reflect upon the essential meaning of their lives. It is often a painful process, sometimes even a cataclysmic one, for it usually entails coming to grips with the myths and absurdities around which one's life has been organized. Moreover, it is a process whose end points are both vague and highly variable. Unlike the poor, where the objectives are clearly to acquire more goods and power, the goals of social intervention with the affluent are much less predictable. For some, it might actually involve divesting themselves of the goods and power accumulated "from the backs of others"; for some, perhaps the majority, it might involve the development of alternative life-styles that are less oppressive and destructive; for still others, it might only result in a heightened awareness of the personal waste that their victories have wrought.[4] In all cases, however, the consciousness-raising experience should, at the very minimum, provide unequivocal data from which continued inaction cannot be rationalized.

However, for all the differences in issues, goals, and strategies, there are areas of substantial similarity in the social intervention work undertaken with both the poor and the affluent. These similarities emerge in what might be called the "mediating processes" through which each group attempts to deal with its own agenda (see Figure 1). By mediating processes we mean those activities which, if undertaken, dealt with, and resolved, form the conceptual link between a group's goals and the social means it develops in order to attain them in ways that lend credibility to the group's psychological and spiritual growth.

Implicit in the orientation presented in this chapter is the notion that, in order for *any* group, whether composed of poor or affluent people, to deal effectively with its pain, it must at some point become involved in two specific tasks. These are the *analysis of contraditions* and the *development of a sense of community*. These tasks, when taken together, comprise the mediating process that links goals and strategies. The analysis of contradictions is nothing more or less than the attempt to develop an ideological framework within which experiences as individuals are first linked and then related to a broader awareness of the purposes of the social order. Thus, for example, when people address themselves to the assumptions underlying a system oriented to goods and power, they are beginning to analyze some of the contradictions that define the social order. When they start to collectively examine the manner in which their lives have been formed and malformed by the myths they have been asked to assimilate about themselves, they are participating in the analysis of contradictions. When they initiate the process of supportive self-criticism they are engaging in the analysis of contradictions.

The analysis of contradictions is, in short, the process by which individuals become united, first by sharing their separate realities and then by going beyond them. The sense of community, on the other hand, is perhaps the most concrete example of what "going beyond separate realities" really entails. It is the development of a new reference group, new in the sense that its members are now free to initiate alternative modes of structuring their relationships, sharing their resources, and organizing their efforts. The sense of community emerges as the result of a uniquely shared historical consciousness. It derives its strength from the willingness of its members to transcend personal agendas; it assumes its meaning to the degree that it provides a model for how people can begin to trust and support one another once it has become clear just how self-defeating the traditional exploitative and competitive ethos really is. It is these two actions, the analysis of contradictions and the development of a sense of community, which in the long run, will determine the conditions under which the poor and the affluent can work together. At present, it is the only thing they really share but they share it unknowingly, for each group has its own pain to contend with and its own agenda it must first realize.

2. Leapfrogging Stages of Economic Development

A second related problem has to do with the tendency of social interventionists to both underrate and undervalue the strivings of people whose class affiliation differs significantly from their own. This is particularly true when, as is so often the case, social interventionists find themselves in situations where they are working with people whose economic position in the social order is well below their own. In part, of course, the phenomenon itself says something about the nature of the human condition insofar as it often seems to be the case that those social interventionists who choose to direct their efforts toward helping the poor are themselves persons whose roots are rarely fixed in the conditions of poverty. For every Cezar Chavez or Harry Bridges whose life and times have been marked by an unwavering commitment to "their people," there are a dozen Robert Kennedys or Mahatma Gandhis whose quest for social justice has placed them in positions of championing the causes of economic groups with which they have few if any direct experiential ties.

The issue, however, is not the validity or utility of social interventionists crossing economic lines in order to render help. To become overly selective about who has the right to help is to be self-defeating: the luxury to choose one's helpers is predicated on the existence of an extensive and readily available pool of manpower and resources, a situation which has never and probably will never be the case with respect to social interventionists.[5] Rather, the issue is one of the degree to which the class-crossing interventionist is conscious of the degree to which his own class background and experiences enter into the immediate situation.

In those instances where the social interventionist comes from a higher socioeconomic group and continues to associate with it, the danger is always present that he will fall prey wittingly or unwittingly to the tendency to ask others to reject that which he has already attained though found wanting. More often than not, this takes the form of urging the disenfranchised to "leapfrog a stage of economic development," not to seek goods and power because of the interventionist's own analysis and experience of their debilitating consequences on the human spirit. "Don't fight so hard for goods and power," he says. "Believe me, I've been there and they're not worth it." "Rather," he continues, "let us focus on what lies beyond goods and power, on the quality of our lives as people seeking a new kind of relatedness and meaning." To be sure, the example offered here borders on the absurd, but its intent is to point out at least two problems that often emerge when the social interventionist working with the poor is, indeed, one whose definition of the American experience is grounded in the voluntary alienation of the affluent. First, there is the tendency to go beyond the people, to succumb to an elitism whose underlying bad faith manifests itself in a profound disregard for the nature and meaning of a disenfranchised group's experience. Second, there is the tendency to romanticize simplicity, to condone someone else's pain, and in the process to disingenuously elevate that pain by imbuing it with a symbolism it never possessed. But, more than anything else, the readiness with which others are urged to forego their class interest bespeaks a critical lack of awareness of the role of economic variables in the progressive liberation and alienation in our society. Roszak (1969), writing with reference to the "counter culture" as opposed to the problems of social intervention, puts the dilemma in the following manner:

> If Allen Ginsberg's *Howl* stands as a founding document of the counter culture, we must remember what the poet had to tell the world: "I have burned all my money in a wastebasket." Will it be a victory, then, or a defeat for the counter culture when the black man has at last fought his way clear of desperate expedients and wrings from the Great Society the white man's equivalent of looting: a steady job, a secure income, easy credit, free access to all the local emporiums, and his own home to pile the merchandise in? The issue is critical because it reveals the bind in which the counter culture finds itself when confronted by undeniably urgent questions of social justice. What, after all, does social justice mean to the outcast and dispossessed? Most obviously it means gaining admission to everything from which middle-class selfishness excludes them. But how does one achieve such admission without simultaneously becoming an integral and supportive element of the technocracy? How do Black Power, black culture, black consciousness stop short of becoming stepping-stones to black consumption, black conformity, black affluence: finally to a middle-class America of another color?
>
> How ready are the workers to disband whole sectors of the industrial apparatus where this proves neces-

sary to achieve ends other than efficient productivity and high consumption? How willing are they to set aside technocratic priorities in favor of a new Simplicity of life, a decelerating social pace, vital leisure? These are questions which enthusiasts of workers' control might do well to ponder. Once the relations of the counter cultural young and the wretched of the earth get beyond the problem of integration, a grave uneasiness is bound to set in. The long-range cultural values of the disconnected young must surely seem bizarre to those whose attention is understandably riveted on sharing the glamorous good things of middle-class life (pp. 67–69).

In a somewhat different but perhaps even clearer manner, the cartoonist Trudeau (Doonesbury) presents the problem (page 115).

In essence, then, the issue boils down to the following question: "As a social interventionist, how do you ask a poor person to give up his desire for a Cadillac because the car will most certainly pollute the air?" The answer is simple: "You don't. You help him get it, all the while trusting that in the process of getting it you will both be able to analyze the contradictions involved and relate those contradicitons to an alternative and future sense of community."

3. Transcending One's Own Socialization

It is much easier to become philosophically and politically opposed to the assumptions underlying a social order, especially one's own, than it is to be free of the effects of having been processed by that social order. The years of socialization, of learning and internalizing the myths and cultural imperatives that eventually come to govern one's life, are not easily overcome; they leave in their wake a powerful legacy of experiential and behavioral predispositions. These predispositions or needs may well be at variance with the

115

long-range goals of social intervention. At their very best they can impede the process of social change; at their very worst they can disable it permanently.

For the social interventionist, the problem of transcending one's own socialization involves a great deal of unlearning, particularly in those areas having to do with ego, status, and control needs. It can only be accomplished to the degree that the interventionist's capacity to be self-critical about his needs in a situation and the social genesis of those needs match his commitment to the aspirations of those with whom he is working. The process of undoing is difficult and is ultimately dependent on the interventionist's ability to use himself as the prime analytical referent. However distasteful he may find the historical consequences of a system predicated on an exploitative individualism, he must acknowledge its subtle impact on his life, particularly as that impact manifests itself in the manner in which he relates to the struggles of others.

The failure to understand and transcend the consequences of one's own socialization appears in many forms. On an individual level it may show itself in a willingness to perpetuate the dependency needs of those with whom one is working, or as Hayden (1973] puts it, to willingly help the powerless to "rule out the possibility that they might be qualified to govern themselves and their own organizations." In such instances the interventionist's ego needs get in the way of group self-determination. They serve to perpetuate an elitist model of leadership. At other times it can take the form of the "lone cowboy" approach to social change. Just like Kissinger's conception of international diplomacy, the interventionist becomes the hired gun, strolling into town at high noon to do battle with the forces of evil. Saul Alinsky gallops into Rochester, shoots it out with the industrial giant (Eastman Kodak), and rides out again amid the cheers of a grateful populace. But what have the people really learned? How stable a form of organizational solidarity remains when

Paladin is gone? Only time will tell, but the record to date is not overly impressive.[6]

Finally, unresolved issues surrounding the interventionist's socialization sometimes surface in the form of inadequate or superficial explanations concerning the meaning of events. In such instances there is the lingering tendency to define issues and problems solely in terms of individuals rather than in terms of broader social forces. A rent strike is directed at a particular landlord or a boycott is carried out against a particular food chain. In both cases the enemy is defined as an individual and the ensuing struggle remains individually oriented. The ultimate relationship of such individuals to the larger institutional and class issues remains a mystery; basic contradictions remain unexamined throughout the process. Whatever victories may be achieved are not related to any developmental or integrated analysis of the corporate forces that each individual represents. They therefore remain short-lived; they do not facilitate further organization; they do not lend themselves to the continuity required for a continuing, cohesive struggle.

On an organizational level, the unexamined issues surrounding one's socialization manifest themselves in one or another form of organizational duplicity, which detracts from the internal moral credibility of an undertaking. In such instances there is a tendency to develop a structure for organizational action characterized by many of the same dynamics and biases as those of the enemy. One need only look at the history of the labor trade-union movement in this country to find evidence of how relatively quickly the attempt to create meaningful change can be transformed into a self-serving corporation with goals and processes virtually indistinguishable from those of its adversaries. The pyramidal allocation of power, individual jockeying for positions of influence, the development of bureaucratic mentality, and the myth that the righteousness of one's cause is of such a magnitude as to automatically offset the importance of other pressing human needs (e.g., group maintenance and support) are but the most obvious examples of this tendency (Sarason, 1972).

More potentially destructive, however, is the possibility that the overall pursuit of social justice can take place at the expense of perpetuating the social injustice of many of a group's original members. For example, as Garofalo (1974) points out, Students for a Democratic Society (SDS) collapsed in 1969, at least in part because of the inability of its warring factions, the Revolutionary Youth Movement and Progressive Labor, to come to grips with the question of the role of women in the movement. We are forced to once again think through the questions surrounding the consequences of a cultural processing.

4. Competition Between "Separate but Equal" Formulations of Oppression

Conditions of weakness and limited resources invariably beget their own offspring, fantasies of imminent strength and solidarity. For social interventionists, the myth of a "united front," of a single movement composed of all of the most obviously oppressed, has always been accorded a special place in the guiding fictions by which sporadic actions take on their meaning. Unfortunately, for all the momentary relief that such fantasies provide, they are self-deluding.

Let us return for a moment to Garofalo's (1974) analysis of the 1969 demise of SDS, for it is an excellent example of what happens when the myth of a united front collapses, when "separate but equal" formulations of oppression come into conflict with each other. Garofalo describes the situation in the following manner:

> In political circles, if not the nation as a whole, the voice of yet another consciousness was beginning to be heard—the women's movement. Tired of simply making coffee, putting out the newsletter, and providing sex after the demonstration, women began rightfully demanding to be treated as equal members of

their respective political organizations. To the extent that equality within male-dominated groups was not forthcoming, the trend among women would parallel the separatism of young blacks.

Describing the plight of politically active black females, Frances Beal (1970), a Student Non-Violent Coordinating Committee (SNCC) field worker, wrote:

> "Since the advent of Black Power, the black male has exerted a more prominent leadership role in our struggle for justice in this country. He sees the System for what it really is, for the most part, but where he rejects its values and mores on many issues, when it comes to women, he seems to take his guidelines from the pages of the *Ladies Home Journal*" (pp. 342–343).

Directed only at black males, the theme, with minor variations, reflected also the feelings of most feminists toward all men.

Without a place to stand and with no visible support community to speak of, political activism on the left was in danger of self-destruction. Nowhere was the deterioration more apparent than the 1969 National Convention of SDS. With more extreme styles, the issues, which divided the organization into the Revolutionary Youth Movement (RYM) faction and the Progressive Labor (PL) faction, had their analogues in every corner of the New Left.

What in SDS was a burning debate over the "national" question, concerning the posture of whites toward black nationalism, was evidenced also in less radical circles in the limited and often precarious alliances among black and white activists. Questions of the "correct" strategy for building an alliance between students and workers had obvious implications for community organizers, including those of a more moderate persuasion. And, questions concerning the equality of women, with implications everywhere, cut across all groups. At the convention, which was already torn by a bitter factionalism, the confirmation of dissonance came when the Black Panther, who was brought in to lend support to the RYM faction, uttered the now infamous line: "The position of women in the revolution is prone." Cries of "Fight Male Chauvinism" rose to a deafening roar and pandemonium reigned. SDS was irrevocably shattered (pp. 8–11).

The basic point, of course, is that there are different, often equally compelling but mutually exclusive, perspectives from which the problems of oppression can be viewed. The belief that there is a single "right" way of ordering the ideological priorities of different groups, that people simply because they are oppressed will automatically define their oppression in ways that are not antagonistic, is to succumb to fantasy. In fact, there are many separate realities, and the failure to understand these distinctive realities usually militates against the development of effective action, especially action of an intergroup variety.

Let us take this book as an example. It should by now be clear that the approach in this book to the problem of oppression is essentially a *class-based approach*. What that means, of course, is that the concept of economic class is the fundamental dimension around which we seek to understand both the original nature as well as the subsequent historical development of the exploitative process. But what that also means is that, since class is conceived as the unifying superordinate theme, questions of race and sex, not to mention age and sexual preference, are necessarily relegated to a subordinate position within the analytical framework. In short, issues of racism and sexism are both contained and subsumed below the imperatives of a class perspective. But that is the reality expressed in this book and no matter how much we are committed to its essential validity, it is not now nor may it ever be the functional reality of black people and of women. For black people, particularly the black male, there is an incontestable experiential legitimacy that makes for a racial view of the world, a perspective within which questions of class and sex become subordinated to issues of color. For feminists, on the other hand, the essence of the oppressive experience is sexual in nature, with class and race assuming a secondary analytical role. While poor people, nonwhites, and women are all oppressed, each group can separately and with compelling justification define the genesis of the oppressive experience to exclude the others in any given struggle.

The logic of this new exclusionism is as unassailable as it is unconscionable but it has happened and will, unfortunately, continue to happen. The movement for women's liberation, for example, is a struggle largely initiated by middle- and upper-class white women, but it also seeks the active involvement of poor black and white women, and it presents poor males, both black and white, as another enemy with which to contend in the course of their own struggle. It also, of course, presents poor women with the problem of choosing between their economic class and their social caste, an unfortunate choice. The situation is not discernibly different (see Figure 2) with respect to struggles involving the self-determination of black people (both rich and poor) and poor people (both black and white).

In each instance, because of the nature of the superordinate imperative around which the social order is analyzed, class versus race versus sex, members of one or another oppressed group will find themselves left out.[7] It is important that the social interventionist understand the rationales for each of the separate but equal formulations, for whether or not they can be brought together or transcended in any particular situation depends, at least in part, on the acceptance of the possibility that oppression, however similarly it may be experienced by poor people, people of color, and women, need not necessarily be interpreted in similar ways.

Figure 2. Separate but Equal Formulations of Oppression: Consequences for Group Inclusion and Exclusion

Superordinate Orientation Toward Oppression

		Class	Race	Sex
Action Consequences	Core Group	Poor People	Non-white People	Females
	Subordinate or Secondary Issues	Race Sex	Sex Class	Class Race
	Excluded Group	Affluent People	White People	Males

The Prospects

If, as we have indicated, the process of change is governed by internal logic, it is also shaped by external realities. These external realities determine, at least to some extent, what it is possible to change in a given situation. Unlike fantasies, these possibilities must be discovered; they do not voluntarly present themselves. Consequently, the search for viable possibilities is as critical to the change process as is the clarity with which a group can articulate its needs, develop an ideology, and evolve a set of values and practices through which it will seek to exercise its collective will.

1. Time Perspective

In a very fundamental sense, the determination of what changes are possible depends on one's analysis not only of how things change, but also *when* things change. One's time perspective is a "phenomenological statement" about the necessary and sufficient conditions under which the combined forces of social history and immediate need meet to produce change. Much as one thinks of the human body as having its internal biological clock, one can view the sweep of history, of culture itself, as conforming to the rhythms of a societal timepiece. Within this rhythm, the relentless ebb and flow of events, social intervention becomes a tinkering process which seeks to hasten the interface of social history and immediate need.

Nowhere are the consequences of one's overall time perspective more obvious than in the determination of what constitutes revolutionary as opposed to evolutionary change. A revolution, for example, is usually defined telescopically: events, much like a whirlpool, are suddenly choked and funneled, driven by their own momentum toward an inevitable and cataclysmic conclusion. The process of evolution, on the other hand, is seen as conclusion-less: the waters seem to meander interminably, their effects only becoming obvious upon inspection of the rocks that have been eroded. Depending on one's limited time perspective, one or the other form of change is imbued with differential virtue: revolution is fast and real while evolution is slow and ephemeral; or revolution is radical and catastrophic while evolution is more in keeping with the natural order of things. What is often forgotten is that both revolution and evolution are as much a part of the same mosaic of change as are the churning whirlpools and sluggish meanderings of any living river.

From our own point of view, the very traditional and narrow definitions of revolution and evolution do little to facilitate the social interventionist's work in a superindustrialized technocracy. Time is now being compacted as never before, at a rate which demands new yardsticks for terms dealing with change. If we contend, as indeed we do, that the traditional conception of revolution is inappropriate for this country, we are not taking a position in favor of moderation or against speed. Rather, we are saying that there does not currently exist either the historical inclination or the degree of class consciousness required for a revolution of the traditional variety. At the same time, it would be less than accurate to view the conditions for change currently being generated by historically excluded groups as typically evolutionary in nature. Indeed, the current separatism, if not polarization, that exists between the women's liberation movement, the Third World movement, and the poor people's movement is a good example of the collapse of most of our categories of thought concerning time and change over time. In each case we see groups striving for self-determination, struggling to deal as quickly as possible with the consequences of a tortured past. Is this revolution? Is the fact that there is not as yet any significant unity between oppressed groups evidence for an evolutionary perspective? Or is it just possible that different groups need time and space in which to develop their identities *before* they turn to the issues which bind them, a position in which the exigencies of time are made to transcend simplistic definitions of evolution and revolution.

It is quite probable that change in this country of the forces behind our goods and power ideology will occur in ways and over a period of time for which there is no existing model. But so long as the social interventionist operates on the basis of a traditional time perspective, so long will he be unable to capitalize on the emergence of new possibilities for acute change in a society increasingly compacted by time.

2. Assumptions About Institutions

The requirements of rhetoric notwithstanding, attempts at social intervention are rarely directed at the conglomerate of forces called "The System." Rather, the attempt is usually made to change a limited but public representation of the system, a particular school, factory, law, or localized set of practices. Specific institutions, therefore, are the primary focus for most interventionist efforts, the assumption being that they not only mirror the larger system but also that whatever works in changing them can be generalized to and have implications for the system as a whole.

The criterion one develops for assessing the success of any attempt to influence or redirect an institution's behavior depends on the assumptions one makes about the manner in which such settings typically change. In turn, the prospects for change, the expectations that guide action, are tied to these assumptions: they invariably influence the planning process, determine the selection of strategies, and provide the dimensions around which a project's success or failure is judged.

Given their place and function in society (see Chapter 3), formal social institutions must be thought of as committed to the maintenance of the broader system they represent. They cannot be expected to embrace or welcome changes which in any way limit their territorial interests or force them to seriously reconsider their presumed legitimacy. In addition, it must be taken for granted that, even in those cases where changes appear to have taken place, there is always the continuing danger of these changes being undone, internally neutralized once the press for change has receded.

Acknowledging the difficulties and limitations involved,

what assumptions can one make about such institutions, particularly with respect to the manner in which they perceive and respond to the forces for change? The first and perhaps most important assumption about institutions is that they are generally *reactive* in nature. Rarely do institutions appear to anticipate, prepare for, or in any other way seek out change on their own. To do so, to be proactive, would imply a commitment to the ongoing examination of one's purpose in the social order, a condition inimical to most socializing and legitimizing institutions. Rather, institutions appear to *respond* to crises, to react to threats or pressures generated from within, or, as is more usually the case, instigated from the outside.

The second assumption has to do with the motives with which institutions approach the necessity of changing some of their practices. If and when an institution changes, it usually changes for both *honest and dishonest reasons*. It is possible, for example, for a social institution, after being confronted with new data concerning the consequences of some of its practices, to change them, make them less patently exclusionary and more responsive to human needs. More often, however, the acceptance of limited change has less to do with the validity of any particular indictment than it does with the institution's desire to ward off larger, more potentially dangerous changes. In such cases, change is accepted for reasons that are primarily political in nature and ultimately self-serving in intent.

The final assumption, somewhat related to the one above, has to do with the amount of change that usually occurs when a setting is altered and the interpretation the social institution places on this change. Change, if and when it takes place, is usually *less* than the amount demanded. Nevertheless, the change is either portrayed to the public as "too much, too soon" or enveloped in rhetoric so ennobling as to lead one to believe that something truly significant has taken place. The social institution that changes, however reluctantly and minimally, is usually accorded the last word in the process, and it exercises this prerogative of the last word to further color the change process to be maximally self-enhancing.

Let us look at a few examples of the process described above. The devastating effects of lead-paint poisoning, particularly in very young children, have been understood for many years. Encephalopathy, irreversible brain damage, paralysis, and death have been known to accompany excessive lead contamination. For those who do not die, there is the specter of lifelong intellectual and emotional handicaps, disabilities which significantly diminish human potential. It is also known that lead poisoning is a man-made problem, a condition traceable to the introduction of lead into the air we breathe, the water we drink, and the food we eat. With respect to children, lead poisoning usually is caused by the ingestion of lead-based paint used in the coating of most dwellings constructed prior to 1940 and still found in many homes, primarily the rented lodgings of low-income families.

Although the causes and consequences of lead-paint poisoning were known for many years, it was not until 1970 that the problem finally became an issue of public concern in the Commonwealth of Massachusetts. The issue was raised by predominantly poor and black parents, whose prior pleas had gone unheeded and whose children had been poisoned, who formed an organization called the Citizens Committee to End Lead Paint Poisoning. It enlisted the support of some concerned professionals and engaged elected officials in a series of confrontations concerning the conditions under which their children were forced to live and die. Amid charges and countercharges between the parents, landlords, and members of various state housing, health, and sanitation agencies, legislation finally was passed in 1971 outlawing the use of lead-based paints and investing the Department of Public Health with the formal mandate of dealing with the problem. Four years later, in 1974, there were still 20,000 poisoning victims and an estimated 75,000 children in a "state of danger" (Bing & Breslin, 1974).

How could this occur? In several ways, all of them illustrative of the assumptions described earlier. To begin with, although the legislation enacted designated the Department of Public Health as the state agency directly responsible for handling the issues surrounding lead-paint poisoning, and although the Department of Public Health responded to escalating pressure for action by creating a Division of Childhood Lead Poisoning Prevention, the new division was both underfunded and left without a director for a full fourteen months.

In other words, the Department of Public Health reacted to the existing hue and cry by demonstrating its concern in symbolic ways, trusting that this would serve to decrease public outrage and adverse publicity. In addition, the new division's definition of the problem was predictably "medico-individual," firmly oriented toward the treatment of existing victims and the prevention of future casualties through the development and coordination of more effective referral, diagnostic, educational, and therapeutic strategies. Finally, given its victim-oriented approach, the new division avoided coming to grips with the real issue involved in the lead-paint poisoning of children: the collusion between landlords and various state regulatory agencies that allowed dangerous, even lethal materials, to be used in the construction and maintenance of the homes of the poor. By treating the problem as a medical problem, focus was directed away from the broader issues of substandard housing and the influence wielded by powerful and monied interests in the running of state government. Indeed, some change had taken place, but it was reactive in nature, far less than actually needed, and ultimately both self-serving and politically inspired in intent.

Another example involves the mental health establishment and centers on the development of the community mental health movement, the so-called bold new approach to prevention and treatment of mental illness. Much as many helping professionals would like to leave the impression that the passage of the Community Mental Health Acts of 1963 and

1964 was due to the forward looking efforts of the mental health industry, the facts are otherwise. By and large, the legislation that gave birth to the community mental health movement was forced upon the professions by events. The socially conscious climate of the decade of the sixties left the mental health professions with no alternative but to take a long, hard look at what they were doing, who they were doing it with, and by implication what they were not doing to alter and influence social conditions. Growing public disquiet concerning the. practices of the mental health establishment forced reflection and brought many professionals face to face with painful and distressing facts that could not easily be dismissed. It was indeed a fact that the poor. in this country had been largely ignored and had become alienated from the mental health professions (Smith & Hobbes, 1966). It was a fact that the poor, even when treated, felt the treatments were irrelevant to their needs and problems (Kelly, 1966). Perhaps most importantly, it was a fact that the mental health professions had traditionally taken a basically passive stance with respect to the social, economic, and institutional inequities that existed in our society (Yolles, 1966), the very conditions which exacted such a heavy toll in human misery and contributed so much to mental health problems. Levine (1967) summarized the situation in the following way:

> The community mental health movement had its origins in a specific set of historical facts and in a set of social and professional pressures. These pressures had to do with the demand for new patterns of treatment which would not remove the mentally ill or the deviant from the community, with the demand for preventive patterns of help, with the inevitable shortage of professionally trained treatment personnel, with dissatisfactions with the efficacy of current patterns of diagnosis and therapy, and with dissatisfactions concerning inequities in the distribution of services to all levels of society (pp. 45).

So much for its origins. But what about the movement itself, this "bold new approach" to the issues of mental illness? Having placed itself on record in favor of change, the mental health professions proceeded in the next ten years to use the rhetoric of community mental health to extend its power, solidify its resources, and guarantee the existence and not insubstantial incomes of more and more traditionally trained professionals. To be sure, some changes occurred. Psychotherapy, for example, was now more available and more liberally dispensed, often at no charge to "inner-city folk." Some interesting attempts were made to develop alternative, nonincarcerative forms of treatment for those previously shipped off to remote, illness-exacerbating mental institutions. Professionals discarded some of their austere garb and obfuscating jargon in favor of mod clothes and "street talk," and forms of community consultation were developed that were somewhat less degrading of clients whose problems and backgrounds were significantly different from those of their helpers. But the changes that took place were largely of the "least common denominator" variety, which only minimally fulfilled the service requirements of the new laws. The changes were designed to insulate from serious reexamination the factors which did not change, and these were the most potentially dangerous aspects of mental health practice: the "blaming the victim" orientation of most approaches to treatment, the increasing tendency of the profession to become allied with society's agencies of citizen control, and the continuing trend toward the separation of questions of mental health and illness from the broader issues of social injustice.

A final example, this time from the field of education, involves the development of black history and black studies programs in the public schools. Once again, external pressure rather than internal initiative was responsible for overcoming institutional inertia. In the case of black history, the pressure came from two directions: from the civil rights movement and from the more generalized cries for educational relevance that characterized the overall atmosphere of the 1960s. Faced with an increasingly strident black population that was becoming more and more enamored with the concepts of Black Power and Black Unity, and knowing full well the serious, long range implications of the community control movement that was beginning to develop, the public schools, heretofore oblivious to the demands by black people for a curriculum showing some concern for questions of black history and black identity, mounted courses in the area of "minority studies." The fact that there was federal money available for such "innovative educational ventures" certainly did little to dampen the public schools' new-found commitment to relevance and improved school-community relations. But the primary intent of these programs had little to do with any serious attempt to explore the meaning and implications of the black experience in America. Teaching black children the birth and death dates of men like Nat Turner and Marcus Garvey, and equating the learning of these facts with acquiring identity, is akin to the belief that white children have been afforded a valid historical perspective by having them incorporate the sanitized profiles of some of the white patriots. What was needed and often demanded was a thoroughgoing reanalysis of the facts and fictions that produce a public history. What was offered was another set of faces and names for students to learn, with little or no attempt to translate this new "material" into any form of altered consciousness. What the introduction of minority studies accomplished was to momentarily take the heat off the public schools, to deflect attention away from the still unchallenged assumptions and ideologies upon which the American educational system is based. There was, indeed, some change, but its extent and meaning remain suspect.

3. Models of Social Intervention

The search for viable avenues of change depends in no small part on the degree to which the social interventionist is committed to the notion that there are multiple pathways to change. There is nothing inherently sacred or pure in being bound to a single view of change. Working within the system has its time and place no differently from working outside the system. Neither approach is of itself ennobling or morally uplifting. Just as there are "different strokes for different folks" with respect to the immediate goals of a particular action, there are different models of action that can be employed to achieve those goals. Effective social intervention is a process requiring both the mastery of a *variety* of intervention strategies and the knowledge of how and when to utilize any one or a combination of those strategies (Goldenberg, 1973).

There are at least three models of change that have been employed by social interventionists. Rarely, however, have these strategies been effectively combined to complement each other. Rather, because of their differing assumptions concerning the nature and conditions for change, they have been viewed as separate and distinct approaches incapable of integration and, therefore, mutually exclusive. The first of these approaches is the *confrontation model.* The confrontation model is predicated on the assumption that different groups have antagonistic and essentially irreconcilable interests, that their needs preclude any mutuality of intent, and that their future, like their past, will be dominated by conflict and coercion. Power is viewed as the necessary and sufficient condition for change, and the process of acquiring, using, and preserving power is the central theme on which strategies and goals are developed. As is the case in any war, battles become sequential in nature, with truces and periodic lulls serving as the context or pretext for suspicion-filled negotiations. Peace is primarily defined in terms of capitulation and the criterion for the effectiveness of any action is its immediate impact on the existing balance of power.

A second approach might be called the *technical assistance model* and is predicated on the assumption that the traditional enmity between groups, between the haves and have-nots, while both understandable and legitimate, need not necessarily preclude the development of communication.

It is a view of the change process that places a premium on the development of skills which facilitate dialogue and negotiation. Problems of oppression are viewed from a perspective that is cross-cultural; based on the assumption that different groups have been so cut off from each others' histories and struggles as to render them foreigners. Consequently, it becomes important that they learn each others' ways, customs, and mores. Whether or not the consequences of history can be undone, the reality of the situation is such that they must develop the skills required for coexistence.

The third model is the *social planning model*. Unlike the confrontation and technical assistance approaches to social intervention, the social planning model is predicated on the assumption that reconciliation is both possible and desirable in the change process. It views the protagonists in any social situation as rational, as persons searching, in their own ways, to do the right thing as best they know how. What is lacking and what the social planning model emphasizes is the ability to transcend the myths and madness that underscore the oppressive experience. Consequently, focus is directed toward the common interests that can bind historically opposing forces. The thrust is oriented to the future, the present situation being viewed as but a stage in the movement toward mutual liberation.

The differences between the models notwithstanding, the prospects for social intervention depend on the interventionist's ability to use whatever approach appears to be most appropriate in any particular situation. What is critical is the awareness that each of the available models of social intervention has its own built-in assets and liabilities and that each brings with it its own assumptions about the nature of change and the relationship between the protagonists in the process of change.

4. The Efficacy of Social Intervention

It is always difficult to assess the impact of any attempt to change the human condition. Unlike most laboratory studies or other experiments in which crucial variables can be easily manipulated, the process of social intervention does not lend itself to the kind of control that can be translated into universally accepted rules and regulations. In the field of social change, whether or not something works often depends on the ways in which conditions come together, in the often unexpected interfacing of issues, moods, and people. Nevertheless, within the unexpected there are certain givens which can be used as predictive anchors for many forms of action.

The efficacy of any attempt to intervene in a social institution depends on the age and stage of development of the target setting. We know, for example, that there is a predictable dynamic that characterizes the life span of any social institution, that its receptivity to change is regulated as much by internal variables as by conditions existing on the outside. Relatively young settings are more amenable to change than are older, more established settings; settings that are fluid, in crisis, or involved in internal upheaval are more immediately vulnerable than are institutions whose operational stability serves as a shield against self-examination. We also know that any social institution, regardless of its public mandate or cultural expectation, goes through at least four stages of development. There is its *innovative stage*, the time during which basic ideologies and modes of practice are worked out. More often than not, this stage is highly fluid in nature and characterized by the expenditure of enormous personal energies and institutional resources. It is followed by a *stage of consolidation*, a relatively long period during which concerns for stability and procedural clarity rule the organization's activities. During such times, especially if the bureaucratization process proceeds unhindered, the setting tends to become organizationally smooth and less open to change independent of source or direction. Sooner or later, however, new crises arise and the setting is forced to reexamine its existing practices and orientations. During such times, when *reflection and rationalization* dominate the day, the institution again becomes vulnerable and fluid, its solidarity threatened both externally and internally. Finally, there is the *stage of renewal or death*, a point at which the institution's history catches up with its future, when prior practices and crises coalesce to mold a new institutional identity. The prospects for effective social intervention are invariably tied to an understanding of the possibilities and problems that each of these stages presents.

A second given has to do with the kind of leverage available to the social interventionist and the amount of credibility he possesses with respect to the setting in which the action is planned. Leverage can be defined in several ways. At one level it can be equated with direct power, the ability to control events. At another level, it refers to influence that is potentially available given the expenditure of time and energy. In both cases, however, leverage involves the notion of *access* and the mobilization of resources that guarantee such access. Where direct access is readily available, the prospects for effective intervention increase; where such access must be developed, where undue time must be spent on the problems of entry, the pospects for change decrease. Credibility, on the other hand, refers to the *seriousness* with which settings view the incursions being mounted against them. To the degree that an intervention can be passed off as a momentary or isolated aberration, as the work of fools, incompetents, or "crazies," to that degree can its legitimacy be undermined for public consumption. The Yippees, for example, could never be taken seriously, either by their institutional adversaries or by those who might have been prepared to support or join them. "Revolution for the hell of it" just couldn't impress those whose oppression was anything but a Sunday lark. The Black Panthers, for all their self-imposed and other problems, were a force to be reckoned with, so much so that the process of their suppression could never proceed smoothly or be fully free from continually labored and increasingly unbelievable justifications (CRIC & Tackwood, 1973).

A final given deals with what might be called the "focus

of an intervention." This refers to the particular institutional point or level at which an action is aimed. Given the complexity and hierarchical nature of most formal social institutions, attempts to introduce change must be predicated on a reasonably sophisticated understanding of the inner workings and patterns of communication that characterize the organization. One could choose to direct one's efforts at improving the skills of certain groups within the setting, or drawing attention to readily apparent ideological contradictions, or dealing directly with the broader constraints under which the setting attempts to wield its influence. The prospects for success in all these cases hinge on understanding the manner in which such intrusions manifest themselves at different levels in the organization. Is it more efficacious to organize the least powerful groups within the system? Or must one always slay the head of the dragon for change to occur? Can change percolate from the bottom up? Or is it invariably the case that changes trickle down from on high? The answers vary from setting to setting: what does not change is the need to assess the traditional character of each setting, to understand the manner in which changes occurring at one level tend to alter the conditions under which business is carried out at other levels.

The Practice

Although the intent of this chapter was not to contribute to the increasing number of handbooks on the practice of social intervention, there are certain issues related to practice that merit consideration. The most important of these has to do with the overriding purpose of almost any intervention whose objective it is to either alter or abolish some particularly oppressive institutional syndrome.

We have already traced the process by which formal social institutions, because of their unique role in the society, transmit and perpetuate the culture's prevailing ideology (see Chapter 3). In addition, we have indicated how unreasonable it would be to expect these institutions to depart, significantly or willingly, from their proscribed social and political functions. Their job is clear: to sustain and monitor a system whose underlying assumptions and technical operations are geared to the exclusion of vast numbers of people. But for these institutions to do their work they must continually develop new rationales for whatever exclusionary practices they are engaged in. They must forever justify their behavior in ways that are consistent with their original mandates.

The process of endless justification requires the constant repackaging of old myths in new containers. This being the case, the practice of social intervention, whatever else its goals and objectives, must always direct itself to the problem of exposing the prevailing myth in the immediate situation. In schools, for example, the myth is usually one involving the nonpolitical character of the educational process and the attendant notion that cultural deprivation or a disorganized nuclear family structure are the basic factors accounting for the inability of children to profit from the educational experience. In the judicial system the myth revolves around the incantation that justice is blind to differences in economic class and skin color. In the area of mental health the myth concerns the absence of any ties between the practices of the helpers and the government's interest in social control. In the fields of welfare and employment the myth involves the assumption that the lack of individual initiative and the reluctance to acquire marketable skills account for the burgeoning welfare and unemployment roles. In each instance, the intent of the myth is to place responsibility squarely on the shoulders of the victim, to perpetuate the image of a basically responsive system unmercifully besieged by incompetent malcontents. Consequently, in each instance the practice of social intervention is incomplete so long as this corporate myth remains unchallenged.

For all its unsettled state, the practice of social intervention need not be disorganized or carried out in ways that appear unduly influenced by passing crises or mercurial shifts in purpose. Indeed, if there is anything which the practice of social intervention should seek to avoid, it is succumbing to the same reactive syndrome that characterizes the response pattern of most of the institutions toward which actions are directed. It is possible, even given all the difficulties involved, such as limited resources, lack of access, undiscovered leverage, and so on, for social intervention to occur in a manner that is both serious and competent. The key to such practice lies in the issues surrounding the timing and sequencing of action.

In those instances where social intervention involves the attempt by traditionally excluded, powerless, and expendable people to collectively alter the conditions under which they live, effective practice depends on the integration of at least five stages of development. These are: first, the mobilization of an informed and risk-oriented core group; second, the identification of the key issues or institutional practices that must be changed; third, the organization of a broader, more powerful constituency; fourth, the development of strategies and the implementation of selected actions together with contingency plans based on anticipated responses of the institution; and fifth, the provision for the maintenance of group unity beyond the period covered by the specific intervention. The sequential nature of these stages is relatively unchanging; what usually varies is the amount of time required to fulfill the criteria for each stage in the process. For example, the completion of stage one, the mobilization of an informed and risk-oriented core group, may involve more time and energy than is usually believed. It is, as Garofalo (1974) points out, a time when people must "get their shit together" and deal with the issues and contradictions of power, leadership, trust, cooperation, and decision making, the core issues around which questons of ideology and community will ultimately be decided. Similarly, with respect to the timing of an action, it is clear that premature political action is almost as ineffective as no action at all. The effective practice of social intervention depends on the degree to which the timing and sequencing of events follows from a clear analysis not only of immediate group needs, but also of the symbolic possibilities and constraints inherent in the undertaking.

Finally, it should be clear that the practice of social intervention, no differently from the analysis which precedes it, can address itself to either or both of the major issues that characterize a society in which exploitation and competition are the means of individual and group survival: it can deal with the immediate problem of the redistribution of existing economic and political resources or it can focus attention on creating the conditions which will question the utility of the goods and power ethos. Both options are usually available but, as we have indicated, the choice ultimately depends on the particular needs of the group involved and its collective experience in the social order. Nevertheless, it is crucial that both options be understood, that they serve as potential sources for intergroup unity and that they not be used to decrease the possibilities of coalition.

In the area of mental health, the formal social institution with which the author is most familiar, the practice of social intervention can address itself to any of a number of issues, each of which could serve the purposes of social change. If, for example, one were primarily interested in trying to stop or significantly retard the tendency of the helping professions to serve the system's exclusionary imperatives, attention might well be directed toward exposing, demystifying, and changing the diagnostic and treatment practices which are used to perpetuate the doctrine of personal culpability. By systematically attacking the "deficit model of help," by making clear the political, social, and economic contradictions upon which it is based, one could question the profession's basic source of allegience. It is important, especially for those whose lives are most adversely affected by the mental health establishment's traditional practices of labeling, separating, and "adjusting" dissidents and deviants, that the profession be made acutely aware of the manner in which such practices have been used to mute and defuse legitimate anger and to divert attention away from any collective analysis of the underlying inequities of the system. Alternately, the practice of social intervention in the arena of mental health might well address itself to the problem of changing the professional priorities that currently determine the allocation of existing resources and manpower. At issue here would be the pressures and forces that have produced a profession committed to the band-aid approach to human problems. At stake would be the attempt to shift the profession away from its traditional affinity for the concept of individual remediation and toward the realization that only by focusing attention and resources on issues of systemic dysfunction can it begin to fulfill its own rhetorical concern for the improvement of the human condition. But, here again, to call into question the manner in which a profession determines its priorities means that the practice of social intervention cannot occur without trying to raise to consciousness issues which many would rather leave untouched. The ultimate resolution of these untouched issues requires personal and professional accountability for which most practitioners are neither prepared nor rewarded. The creation of the conditions that nurture such accountability is a valid goal of any attempt at social intervention.

For those who have no power, salvation is usually defined in terms of its acquisition; for those who have power, salvation may very well lie in giving it up. In both instances the historical process that has made power the fulcrum around which the existential drama is played out remains unchallenged and unchanged. All attempts at altering the human condition take place against this background. The process of social intervention cannot undo the past; it can only seek to reshape the present and influence the future. To the degree, however, that it does not understand the past, that it is not humbled by history, to that degree will it give sustenance to those who hold the grimmest views of our ultimate destiny. It is in this sense that the problems, prospects, and practice of social intervention take on a special meaning. And it is that special meaning that we have sought to convey in this chapter.

5

The New Conservatives

A nation, particularly its young people, sings its consciousness. Its songs tell us something about ourselves and the times we live in.

In 1965 we looked at the world and at each other and sang with anger and determination, our voices echoing the outrage of unfulfilled promises. It was the *Eve of Destruction* and our words were no less clear than our implied resolve to "right the unrightable wrongs" that had so marred the human condition.

> The eastern world, it is explodin',
> Violence flarin' and bullets loadin',
> You're old enough to kill,
> But not for votin',
> You don't believe in war,
> But what's that gun you're totin'?
> And even Jordan River has bodies floatin'!

Don't you understand what I'm try'n to say?
Can't you feel the fear that I'm feelin' today?
If the button is pushed there's no running away.
There'll be no one to save
With the world in a grave.
Take a look around you, boy,
It's bound to scare you boy.

My blood's so mad feels like coagulatin',
I'm sittin' here just contemplatin'.
You can't twist the truth, it knows no regulatin',
And a handful of Senators don't pass legislation,
Marches alone can't bring integration,
When human respect is disintegratin'.
The whole crazy world is just too frustratin'.

Think of all the hate there is in Red China,
Then take a look around to Selma, Alabama!
You may leave here for four days in space,
But when you return, it's the same old place.
The pounding drums, the pride and disgrace,
You can bury your dead, but don't leave a trace,
Hate your next door neighbor, but don't forget to
    say grace.

Tell me over and over and over again my friend,
Ah, don't you believe we're on the EVE OF
DESTRUCTION.

Now, ten years later, we sing very different songs, songs
that neither go out of their way to condemn the forces of
tyranny nor seek to draw any parallels between "Red China
and Selma, Alabama." Rather, our songs now bespeak a certain resignation to "the day the music died" (*American Pie*),
an acceptance of limited possibilities for the fulfillment of old
dreams (*Me and Mrs. Jones*), and a newfound splendor in the
nostalgic past (*Yesterday Once More*). It is a time for
"wringing the truth out of jive," for recoiling from the wan-

ing urges to change the world, for focusing instead on the re-discovery of the soul and the pursuit of the elusive love "that makes us go on" (*Back When My Hair Was Short*). Our hair may or may not be getting shorter, but our songs are less strident, our consciousness' more personalized, and our exis-tence more subdued and firmly anchored in the individu-alized pursuit of a calming or frenetic autonomy. We look at the past, smile at our misspent energies, and walk away from the unrealized hopes. We have become convinced that sur-vival, rather than salvation, is the meaning of our existence.

> Back when my hair was short,
> I was a white-sock sport;
> Wore pointed shoes and pegged pants;
> Drank till my eyes were red,
> Hid *Playboy* beneath my bed;
> And dreamed about love.
> We were experts on love;
> We talked our way all around it.
> And even if we found it,
> We couldn't respond.
>
> Slowly I changed my ways,
> College and long-hair days;
> Seeing three concerts a week,
> An honest-to-God hippie freak,
> Too busy eating to speak,
> Except about love.
> We held rallies for love,
> But no one knew what they stood for.
> How many months were they good for,
> The meaning is gone.
>
> Soon when my hair is short,
> I'll make a full report
> Of how I came back alive,
> And what it takes to survive.
> Wringing the truth out of jive.

> I'll tell you of love,
> More than ever it's love.
> No lack of faith undermines it,
> Because it's the hope that we'll find it
> That makes us go on.

The atmosphere and settings in which our songs are sung have changed. The almost reverential tone of a Joan Baez concert has been replaced by the macabre and sado-masochistic frenzy of an Alice Cooper happening. Instead of locking arms to let the world know that *We Shall Overcome,* we now sit transfixed, endlessly chanting our "oms" into the fluid abyss or gazing vacantly through the vibrations of an electrified emptiness whose fury is as numbing as the drugs we take to endure it. It is, indeed, a new day: a day in which Jerry Rubin sings of the glories of bioenergetics, western sunshine, and good vibes; a day in which Rennie Davis prostrates himself before a sixteen-year-old ulcerative guru. The "Great White Hopes" have left the ring; and many of their black compatriots are either civilizing white America while holed up in expensive California suites or resolutely doing breadbasket business with the banks of Mayor Daley's Chicago. We seem, as Hayes (1969) put it, to have "smiled through the apocalypse..." and come up empty.

> Now for ten years we've been on our own,
> And moss grows fat on a rollin' stone,
> But that's not how it used to be
> When the jester sang for the king and queen
> In a coat he borrowed from James Dean
> And a voice that came from you and me,
> Oh, and while the king was looking down,
> The jester stole his thorny crown.
> The courtroom was adjourned,
> No verdict was returned.
> And while Lennon read a book on Marx
> The quartet practiced in the park
> And we sang dirges in the dark
> The day the music died. (*American Pie*)

Just when did the music die? For some it died when the instant intimacy of Woodstock was transformed into the grotesque horror of Altamont. For others it happened at the 1968 Democratic National Convention in a little park suddenly and forever famous because of the unrestrained cruelty of its uniformed defenders (Genet, 1969). For still others the death knell was sounded a long time ago, in the dim and receding glimmers of the past, on "the night they burned old Dixie down."

But whatever the time, the fact of the matter is that in a very real sense *we are today a people and a country who have become frightened by our violence and depressed by our impotence* (Goldenberg, 1972). And it is this reality that must be understood, for it has both robbed the cause of social intervention of many of its most potentially able and forceful white participants and has, in their stead bred a brand of *New Conservativism* which promises precious little in the way of support for the unfinished struggles of our day. Consequently, the purpose of this chapter is threefold: first, to examine our not very distant past in the hope that we will understand the manner in which the magnitude of our recent memories is shaping our current behavior; second, to isolate the core issues around which our experiences and choices are organized; and finally, to explore the ways in which these experiences are being expressed to further impede the process of social change. And, as is so often the case in biased forays into psychohistorical analysis, our goal is not simply to understand the past; it is to comprehend the separate experiential threads out of which we must weave a different future.

America:
Our Recent Past and Contemporary Life-Styles

The events of the 1960s placed squarely before this nation the nature and extent of America's unfinished business. Poverty, racism, sexism, and violence are the myriad causes, manifestations, and consequences of one or another form of growth-inhibiting oppression. They were exposed before the public with an intensity previously unknown or only dimly approximated. The data were clear and compelling. A significant proportion of America's citizenry was actively and consciously prevented from exploring and realizing the full limits of their creative potential. In addition, those not actively engaged in preventing were themselves dehumanized by virtue of their nonresistance to the process that was destroying others. The effects on the human spirit were profound. As previously indicated (see Chapter 1), for both the affluent as well as the poor there was a loss of self, a feeling of rage coupled with powerlessness, and an overwhelming sense of futility, of being controlled and regulated by an often impersonalized and increasingly computerized system fast approaching madness. The decay of the cities was rivaled only by the barrenness of the suburbs. There was, indeed, some limited continuity between the numbing life in our urban, rat-infested ghettos and the ostrichlike existence that scrawled its empty message over the manicured lawns of our middle-American Similarsburgs and Lookalikesvilles. In both cases, the symptoms of a disordered and disorienting existence were overly abundant: withdrawal, violence, and despair were as deeply rooted in the American landscape as any cancer eating away at the waning vitality of a living organism.

But, even amidst these problems, the early 1960s were years of hope. If there was much that was rotten in America, there was also something that was coming alive, something struggling to respond to events with a newfound sense of urgency bordering on exhilaration (McReynolds, 1971). To begin with, we had a new president, a young man who, as one historian (Schlesinger, 1965) put it:

> ... voiced the disquietude of the postwar generation—the mistrust of rhetoric, the disdain for pomposity, the impatience with the postures and pieties of other days, the resignation to disappointment. And he also voiced the new generation's longings ... for a link between past and future, for adventure and valor and honor (p. 114).

In short, we had a leader whose style promised much, not the least of which was the vision (certainly the rhetoric) that we could start anew to create a society that was more rational, liberating, and worthy of its people.

> I do not want it said of our generation what T. S. Eliot wrote in his poem, *The Rock*—"and the wind shall say these were decent people, their only monument the asphalt road and a thousand lost golf balls." (John F. Kennedy, Columbus, Ohio, October 17, 1960)

But we had more than a leader. We had the prospects of new federal progress like the War on Poverty (passed after JFK's assassination) which would inaugurate an era of massive human and institutional renewal. It was an era founded on the assumption that this country, given its historical gestures and traditions of social reform, could once again marshall its resources to deal simultaneously with both the victims of the system as well as the institutional sources of their victimization. It was, in short, a time when the long-dormant voices of Woody Guthrie and Cisco Houston would once again rise up from their graves in the dustbowls and Hoovervilles of a bygone age, sweep across the years and miles, and speak to a new generation of Americans. Only now their songs were translated into the idiom and styles of the 1960s, and their voices had new faces, Murray the K and James Brown joined Hubert Humphrey and R. Sargent Shriver in a chorus of *You're What's Happening, Baby*, each singing in his own key to his own audience but all employing the same basic theme of Right Now!, the future . . . and hope.

And so, the decade of the sixties began with purpose only to end with pain. For a few highly visible moments America seemed poised, ready to undertake the awesome task of transcending its own historical consciousness. But instead, almost as if guided by a faceless archetypical reflex, it recoiled from the existential moment and destroyed the very ones who symbolized its approaching liberation. First John F. Kennedy, then Martin Luther King, then Malcolm X, and finally Robert F. Kenndey—prophets all, in a land needing redemption—were gone. It was the death of charisma. *And it was then, with their executions, that we were finally confronted with the immenseness of the violence that lies at the heart of the American experience. And we became afraid.*

And what of the programs of the sixties? The War on Poverty, we soon found out, was never really intended to be a war at all. We had again been deceived, our energies sapped by yet another empty ritual. At its very best the War on Poverty was a painfully timid and overly self-conscious assault on the consequences rather than the causes of human misery. To be sure, some used it to carve out new careers for themselves in the massive helping conglomerates and consultant firms that siphoned off the peoples' resources. Others were left untouched by its existence. But, even so, the war that never was a war became its own first casualty. The program whose only goal was to reaffirm the American Dream became the victim of the very system it sought to canonize. *And so we were confronted with our own impotence to create rapid and meaningful social change in a land as complex and divided as ours. And we became depressed.*

And so today, in 1978, our choices for how we wish to lead our lives are in one way or another being shaped by the images and memories of our recent past. How much are we willing to risk when our recent past tells us that those, like the prophets and near-prophets of the sixties, who are willing to risk can be summarily destroyed? How much are we willing to commit ourselves to the agonizing process of social change when our recent past tells us that such commitments often result in despair and disillusionment. In short, what guiding fictions shall we adopt in the attempt to give our lives a semblance of meaning in a world that increasingly defies description?

For too many, those we shall call the *New Conservatives,* the events of the sixties were shattering beyond description. They had stared into the Forbidden, had seen the seething cauldron in which the Beast lurked, and were overwhelmed by its naked fury. It would not respond to logic. It did not understand moral injunctions. It was only faintly amused by political polemics. But when approached, however righteously or cautiously, it lashed out with a venom whose force and finality was as searing as any shock wave conjured up from the Deep. It could maim, or kill, or neutralize; but more than anything else it could drain the vitality and passion out of virgin ideals and untested idealists. As Lester (1968) put it:

> They found out what blacks have always been aware of—that America is the country where Love was killed. They have grown up believing that their country was good and kind and that they, because they could "vote for the candidate of their choice" were participants in governing their lives. It has come as a shock to them to learn that their country is not good, not kind, and that they have absolutely no power to change anything. The existing Power maintains itself through rhetoric and force (pp. 120–121).

With the lessons of the sixties still fresh and burning in their memories, many of the fledgling social combatants turned and ran, removed themselves from the frightening realities, sought solace and comfort in anarchic individualism —and became the New Conservatives. As the New Conservatives, they now point to the world and what it has done to people and conclude that it is a patently absurd place and totally unchangeable. They look at values and people as essentially transient, replaceable, and no longer capable of evoking or demanding long-term commitments. For those who have adopted the life-style of the New Conservatives there will be little if any direct engagement with the world. The New Conservatives will not allow themselves to be seduced or fall prey to social causes of any kind, for they recall all too clearly the meager results of the movements for social justice in the sixties. Instead, they withdraw from the world, secure in the presumptive knowledge that the only change over which there is any hope of direct control is the change that occurs within themselves. Clearly, the only legitimate revolution is in the head. Therefore, they focus all of their efforts on themselves, on perfecting their personal sensitivity and opening themselves up to the wonders of an increasingly romanticized spontaneity about the world and the individuals who happen through it. They build temporary societies and communes devoted to organic farming or exploring the limits of sexuality and "relating" in a setting where revolution is defined as the elimination of sex-role stereotyping. Or they become protean beings capable of flowing in and out of a variety of settings, people endlessly in pursuit of novelty, people "doing their own thing," bound together solely by the shared conviction that social movements are not only dangerous and intrusive, but ultimately useless. But whatever they do, and much of it is beautiful or, at least, wrapped in beautiful rhetoric, their first and last allegiance will always be toward themselves and their infinite perfection and raised consciousness as human beings.[1]

Luckily, there are always instant prophets available to lend an air of respectability for almost any undertaking. For the New Conservatives, the kind of social withdrawal they have elected to equate with superior purpose has found its philosophical and psychological legitimation in the likes of Charles Reich and Frederick Perls. From the work of Reich (1970) has come the necessary social analysis out of which a "soft revolution" (von Hoffman, 1970) emerges not only as desirable, but also as gloriously credible. And whether or not Marcuse (1970) dubs it as "the Establishment version of the great rebellion," or Ways (1970) sees in "Consciousness III" a new way of making the "Corporate State" more palatable to the young, the *Greening of America* has succeeded in transforming escapism into a cultural heroism of truly impressive dimensions.[2] From Perls (1971), on the other hand, the New Conservatives have received the kind of imprecise humanistic annointment so necessary in turning political and social disengagement into a mental health celebration. More-

over, they have been given a *Gestalt Prayer* to mutter as
they bob and weave their way through the ruins of a non-
humanistic society.

It is difficult to calculate, at least at this point, just how
deeply the New Conservativism has become ingrained in the
collective soul of our young people. It is also difficult to project the long term consequences of this new turning away
and turning inward. What is fairly obvious is that the New
Conservativism has torn precious person-power from the
ranks of the social activists. But what is most unavoidable
is the conclusion that there is a cause and effect relationship
between the events of the sixties and the timidity which
some might call the gentleness of the seventies. Clearly, our
recent past is still reverberating within us.

The Core Issue: Loss of Control

It would be a mistake of immense proportions to view
the disengagement of the New Conservatives as a totally
unique and unprecedented response to social crisis. To be
sure, certain aspects of their disaffection have taken a form
for which there are few cultural analogs, but, from a social
interventionist perspective, the specifics of the current
"withdrawal from the world" are far less important than the
isolation of that underlying issue around which life-styles
became shaped and reshaped. The New Conservatives are not
alone in their attempts to negotiate their way through and
around the increasingly complex matrix we call the social order. They are merely the latest group to deal with that unresolved issue—*the loss of control*—which has both dominated
and plagued the last thirty years of this American century.

It is our thesis that, although the entire history of the
human species can be viewed from the perspective of man's
ongoing attempt to assert his dominion over the natural
world, a single critical event—the atomic bomb—so changed
the nature of this struggle as to place the question of control
in a bold relief from which it has never really receded. While

it may be considered passé to focus attention on the lingering consequences of Hiroshima and Nagasaki, it is our belief that the psychological impact of those events so altered our conception of control, so increased our sense of having lost it and placed in such doubt our ability of ever regaining it, as to significantly influence the last three decades of our existence both as individuals and as a people.

It is almost impossible to describe what the dropping of the atomic bomb must have signified to the ages. In one bloody mushroom we demonstrated: *first, that as a collectivity we now controlled the very elements out of which we had sprung; and second, that as individuals we could no longer indulge in the belief that we had any control over our destinies.* In a single apocalyptic moment we both conquered the heavens and became the first casualties of our Pyrrhic victory. The incineration was complete: the ultimate long-range psychological consequences were to be almost as devastating as the torn and mutilated remains of those for whom the sun had exploded.

In a very real sense, the last thirty years of our mode of being in this country can be viewed as a series of discrete but related attempts to deal with the psychological consequences of the loss of control. Even more than the guilt associated with having been the country that committed the unthinkable and dropped the atomic bomb, our recent past, especially since 1945, has been influenced by the problems and pressures of trying to come to grips with the loss of control symbolized by the moral, ethical, and technological issues surrounding our national power on the one hand, and by the growing reality of our concomitant personal impotence on the other. The life-styles we have developed in the fifties, the sixties, and in the current decade can be characterized and perhaps understood as ways of trying to recapture a sense of ownership over our lives, as ways of either adjusting or trying to reassert our dominion over the events which robbed us of our feigned immortality.

In the fifties, during the decade immediately following the event of the bomb, when memories were freshest and most difficult to deal with, we developed the appropriate life-styles which sought to deny the bomb's impact. It was truly a period of quiet desperation. It was a time of dullness and Dulles, mistrust and Joe McCarthy, tailfins and torpor, security-seeking, and, above all else, silence. We became a people who either joined in the endless quest for status or withdrew into purposely disorganized bands of muted rebels and quiet insurrectionists. Schlesinger (1965) described well this "generation which had experienced nothing but turbulence":

> ... in the fifties some sought security at the expense of identity and became organization men. Others sought identity at the expense of security and became beatniks. Each course created only a partial man (pp. 113–114).

The affluent years were upon us and those who became members of *The Lonely Crowd* (Riesman, Glazer & Denny, 1950) or *The Status Seekers* (Packard, 1959) sought in their new suburbs and packaged villages that measure of security and permanence that the world situation could no longer offer or pretend to guarantee. These were the "organization men," who, being denied a sense of historical continuity, reached out for the instantaneous "belongingness" offered them by the assumedly beneficent organization. Whyte (1959) put it this way:

> Listen to them talk to each other over the front lawns of their suburbia and you cannot help but be struck by how well they grasp the common denominators which bind them. Whatever the differences in their organization ties, it is the common problems of collective work that dominate their attentions, and when the DuPont man talks to the research chemist or the

chemist to the army man, it is these problems that are uppermost. The word "collective" most of them can't bring themselves to use—except to describe foreign countries or organizations they don't work for—but they are keenly aware of how much more deeply beholden they are to organizations than were their elders. They are wry about it, to be sure; they talk of the "treadmill," the "rat race," of the inability to control one's direction. But they have no great sense of plight; between themselves and organization they believe they see an ultimate harmony and, more than most elders recognize, they are building an ideology that will vouchsafe this trust (p. 4).

Other, those few who chose the not so quiet refuge offered by Kerouac's *Subterraneans* (1959) and Lipton's *Holy Barbarians* (1959), sought "nonalignment" and became the alienated hipster the precursor of our New Conservatives who, as Holmes (1960) described it:

... moves through our cities like a member of some mysterious, nonviolent Underground, not plotting anything, but merely keeping alive an unpopular philosophy, much like the Christian of the first century. He finds in bop, the milder narcotics, his secretive language and the night itself, affirmation of an individuality (more and more besieged by the conformity of our national life), which can sometimes only be expressed by outright eccentricity. But his aim is to be asocial, not anti-social; his trancelike "digging" of jazz or sex or marijuana is an effort to free himself, not exert power over others. In his most enlightened state, the hipster feels that argument, violence, and concern for attachments are ultimately Square, and he says, "Yes, man, yes!" to the Buddhist principle that most human miseries arise from these emotions. I once heard a young hipster exclaim wearily to the antagonist in a barroom brawl: "Oh, man, you don't want to interfere with him, with his kick. I mean, man, what a drag!"

On this level, the hipster practices a kind of passive resistance to the Square society in which he lives, and the most he would ever propose as a program would be the removal of every social and intellectual restraint to the expression and enjoyment of his unique individuality, and the "kicks" of "digging" life through it (pp. 18–19).

Schlesinger (1965), perhaps better than anyone else, captured the essential quality of the fifties; he described it in the following way:

> In the fifties the young men and women of the nation seemed to fall into two groups. The vast majority were the "silent generation," the "careful young men," the "men in the gray flannel suits"—a generation fearful of politics, incurious about society, mistrustful of ideas, desperate about personal security. A small majority, rejecting the respectable world as absurd, defected from it and became beats and hipsters, "rebels without a cause." Pervading both groups was a profound sense of impotence—a feeling that the social order had to be taken as a whole or repudiated as a whole and was beyond the power of the individual to change. David Riesman, hearing undergraduate complaints in the late fifties, wrote, "When I ask such students what they have done about these things, they were surprised at the very thought they could do anything. They think I am joking when I suggest that, if things came to the worst, they could picket! ... It seems to me that their activities might make a difference, because, in a way, they profit from their lack of commitment to what they are doing" (pp. 739–740).

The fifties then, were a time when people, particularly

young people, acutely aware of how personally helpless they had been rendered by the awesome nature of their own and their elders' technological creativity, sought to develop ways of handling their newfound expendability. The sun had burst over Hiroshima and Nagasaki; now, given the madmen who might come to inhabit the White House or the Kremlin, it could just as easily mute the stars over New York or Peoria. It was not our fingers that would steady the button, but it was our existence that would be obliterated if and when it was pushed. A nation had developed the bomb, but a single human being could now trigger it. What greater basis could there be for feeling that one's fate was no longer in one's own hands. And so the life-styles that eventually developed, conformity and silence on the one hand and aimless wandering on the other, were our responses to this loss of control. In the former instance, it took the guise of an instant and artificial immortality characterized by possessions, things, and a "proper organizational attitude" to create or recapture a feeling of permanence, belonging, and security. In the latter case, it took the form of a nomadic pursuit of a variety of experiences that could only be trapped after the demands and commitments symbolized by the square world had been relinquished. If doomsday was just around the corner, why feign any interest in proper burials?

If the fifties were silent years, the decade of the sixties sought its roots in action.[3] Fifteen years had come and gone since the bomb had made its debut—and we were still around. Slowly but surely a people stopped both preparing for death and pretending that it would never come. It finally dawned on us that while we were frantically building and burrowing into our bomb shelters or getting stoned "on the road," others were busily taking care of earthly business in ways that were frightening. We felt that enough time had passed since that fateful day in 1945. We had had enough time to accept the reality of the unthinkable; we had had fifteen years to adjust ourselves to the possibilities of the supposedly final maelstrom, and we were now once again becoming free to concern ourselves anew with the conditions under which we waited. If we could not control the time and place of our death, we could at least try to reassert our dominion over the quality of our lives. However fragile and uncontrollable the future might be, the present was ours to shape, to stamp with a rationality as impressive as the irrationality that surrounded it.

Therefore, the sixties began as a time when personal visibility, social responsibility, and the quest for a self-critical autonomy began to replace the aimless and egocentric quietude of the previous decade. America was entering a new decade, and its entrance was giving birth and form to a new style, an altered orientation, and a new perspective in the conduct of public affairs. The nation began to examine itself with greater objectivity and candor and to understand how great a discrepancy there was between the image it tried to project abroad and the harsh imperfections of the society within its own borders. The doubting and challenging of institutions and established ways of thinking were no longer luxuries and were no longer interpreted as acts of treason: they became an imperative, an obligation, a sacred trust. There was now nothing inherently wrong with being imperfect, either as an individual or as a nation. What was morally wrong was the inability to admit imperfection and the unwillingness to do anything about it. Thought became coupled with personal action, and a nation of young people began to understand that taking risks and accepting perils in the service of ideals were the causes, rather than the effects, of freedom. More than anything else, a generation of Americans viewed themselves as cheated so long as they lived in a society which for all its affluence and wealth was still incomplete and unfinished.

The atmosphere that was once again making individual action meaningful, an atmosphere in which, as Schlesinger (1965) put it, "even picketing no longer appeared so ludicrous or futile," was also infusing old movements with a new and youthful dynamism that elders found at once both awe-inspiring and a little frightening. College campuses once again began seething with political and intellectual unrest, and the movement for civil and human rights was born anew. In both cases there was a new instance and an impatience to wait the amount of time that had so often in the past resulted in the conversion and subversion of high ideals into more mature forms of reflection and nonaction. The concepts of partial fulfillment, half-victories, and "wait, take your time, don't go too fast" were relegated to the past, to the dunghill of worn-out ideas: "Freedom Now!" was the chant of the present.

The early 1960s was a time when direct action became the vehicle and a life-style for the attainment of individual and group identity, autonomy, and fulfillment. Selfhood was now defined in terms of one's willingness and ability to act, and through this action to alter and influence the human condition. It was a time when three young men (Michael Schwerner, Andrew Goodman, and James Chaney) would die, not only *with* but *for* each other, realizing that what bound them together was a morality that transcended time and place.

But, as we have already indicated, *death and disappointment, together with the fear and impotence they engendered, conspired to short-circuit a life-style in which personal growth became synonymous with social change.* The questions surrounding control had not been dealt with in any satisfying manner. The seeds were now sown for the New Conservatives of the seventies. The ground was ready for them to blossom.

Attempts to Reassert Control: The New Conservatives in "Action"

It should be clear that when we speak of the New Conservatives we are not referring to any single group. Rather we are calling attention to a specific *attitude* both toward the world and to the issues associated with change. The attitude is one in which the dual problems of control and change are increasingly personalized, projected onto a much smaller screen, deflected away from the broader society, and focused much more intensely on those limited aspects of the universe which are deemed manageable, the self and the smaller amalgams in which one tries to live. The orientation is such that the exploration of the self and the limits of individual tolerance become the fulcrum on which the issues of control and change continually revolve.

Unlike the organizational men of the fifties, the New Conservatives view social status and material security as debilitating; unlike the subterraneans of the fifties, loneliness is not equated with virtue; and unlike the social activists of the sixties, there is no presumption of any identity between one's sense of incompleteness and the imperfections of the human condition. If one has decided that one cannot change the world and yet refuses to be changed by it—if one relishes one's uniqueness and yet derives no great joy in its solitary pursuit—if, in short, one's definition of control falls somewhere in between conquest and surrender, then issues of survival can be imbued with a new meaning and a new rhetoric that produces an instant ideology. For the New Conservatives this ideology is a *Not Quite Ideology*. They are committed, but not quite; they are alienated, but not quite; they are "into" themselves, but not quite; they are "into" being with others, but not quite. They are at one and the same time fearful of traditional social engagement and mortified of interpersonal estrangement. Fundamentally, however, as was the case with respect to their predecessors, the question of control remains the primary issue that must be resolved: for the New Conservatives the resolution has taken a variety of forms, all of them oriented toward a salvation that is almost exclusively individualistic.

1. Sensitivity: The Glorious Quest

It is no accident that the development and proliferation of the sensitivity movement in all of its forms and with all of its myriad offshoots, sects, fads, and cults should so closely parallel the evolution of the New Conservative form of political and social disengagement.[4] The movement, for all its flowery rhetoric and impassioned purpose, is predicated on the *assumption that problems are fundamentally personal and interpersonal in nature and that the only kinds of changes that are either possible or worth one's efforts are those which are limited to the areas of interpersonal and small group behavior*. Indeed, no less a figure than Carl Rogers, a towering force and a proponent of the "Human Potentials movement," believes that "intensive group experiences are perhaps the most significant social invention of this century" (Darrach, 1970). Such legitimation is hard to come by, and, although Rogers' assertion is historically incorrect, it attests to the effort being expended to cloak the movement in the garb of a scientific or humanistic breakthrough.

Since 1947, when the first National Training Laboratory was established in Bethel, Maine, a large and increasing number of social scientists and educated laymen entered into the T-group era, the age of the "laboratory approach to reeducation" (Bradford, Gibb & Benne, 1964). To its advocates, sensitivity training represents a unique opportunity through which the resources of the behavioral sciences and the values and needs of a democratic society can be united and can form a reciprocal working relationship. From this point of view, the sensitivity workshop becomes a setting that affords its members the opportunity of learning about themselves, improving their interpersonal skills, and joining with one another in the quest for rational solutions to personal, interpersonal, and group problems. To its detractors (this writer included, obviously), the sensitivity movement is a game, a cop-out, however intellectually rationalized and scientifically fortified it might appear. For this group of critics, sensitivity training represents little more than the cultivation of those palaverous skills which allow, indeed enable and reward, those who might otherwise seek to create real social change to live with the status quo and to accept their impotence and powerlessness with a modicum of dignity.

For the New Conservatives, the pursuit of an ever-increasing individual sensitivity has transformed winter into an endless summer. From encounter groups to marathons, from emergent groups to authenticity groups, from embedded groups to microexperiences, from weekend sensitivity retreats (increasingly a part of the Catskill resorts' shill to garner the trade of "singles of all ages") to creativity-growth labs, from inquiry groups to nude sharings in the sauna bath, and from "uprooting and rerouting" groups to just plain old T-groups, the possibilities for momentary intimacy are almost as abundant and numerous as the people prepared to "reach out" for them. And they are indeed reaching out, answering the call to make contact, to *Please Touch* (Howard, 1970). According to Gibb (1970):

> The growth of sensitivity training throughout the world in the past two decades has become a notable cultural phenomenon. The method has become a basic element in programs of teacher training, therapy, executive development, personal growth, group counselling, sex education, community mental health, treatment of drug addicts and alcoholics, family counselling, organizational change, recreation, social work, vocational rehabilitation and formal education.
>
> Since the method was used by the National Training Laboratories in 1947, something like three-quarters of a million participants have had an intensive experience in some kind of sensitivity group. Indicative of the potential impact of such training upon contemporary life is the fact that the large proportion of participants have been people in responsible roles in industry, government, the churches, the schools, and voluntary organizations (pp. 6-7).

It does not seem to matter that there is no unequivocal evidence attesting to the effectiveness, even in terms of results for individuals of the movement (Lieberman, Yalom & Miles, 1973), that there are serious ethical questions surrounding its use (Lakin, 1969), and that abuses of the method are both well known and widespread (Winthrop, 1971). Nor does it seem to make any difference that the movement's techniques, far from being aimed at liberating individuals, were originally developed and continue to be used, although in disguised forms, for the explicit purpose of increasing worker productivity by manipulating the conditions of labor (e.g., the 1930s Roethlisberger and Dickson "Hawthorne Experiments" at the Western Electric Company). The temporary "high" of the experience is apparently enough to offset questions of validity, ethics, abuse, and accountability (Maliver, 1971).

But there is much more to the sensitivity movement that accounts for its attractiveness. And there is more to it to attest to its danger. Its attraction is rooted in the illusion it offers its seekers of a new and meaningful way of gaining control over their lives. First, by defining problems in personal and interpersonal terms, it orients individuals away from the larger society and away from the forces that proved so implacable just a few short years ago; and second, it provides intensive but reasonably safe and socially supported simulations through which they can act out their existential despair. They do so through games like Blind-Leading, Talk-to-Your-Headache, Breaking-Out, Group-Grope, High Noon, Falling, and so on. The movement projects an aura of possibilities, a feeling, if not of instant mastery, at least of irreversible growth and "unfolding."

The dangers of the glorious quest stem directly from its attractions. Its implicit ideology is patently individuo-narcissistic, and its methodology is clearly deceiving. Consequently, it is not surprising to find the movement making inroads in our formal social institutions, such as our schools, churches, helping agencies, industry, and the government itself. It results in a brand of creative withdrawal and submission under the guise of increased personal freedom that is tailor-made to the needs of a social system that seeks to avoid careful analysis and neutralize organized discontent. Indeed, it is so pervasive that if a hypothetical tyrant wanted to guarantee that there would be no real opposition to his beliefs and practices, he could succeed by passing a law mandating that all of his subjects participate in an encounter group at least twice a week.

2. Behavior Modification: Instant Competence

The surge of interest in the application of learning theory principles to the problems of human behavior is the only recent development within the social sciences that appears to threaten, both in its appeal and in its ability to win converts, the steady advance of the sensitivity movement. It would appear, at least on the surface, that no two orientations could be as dissimilar or as antagonistic toward each other than those represented by the sensitivity movement and the assorted group of practices known as "behavior modification." There are, to be sure, some very real and significant differences between the two approaches: the behavior mod people pride themselves on their objectivity, precision, and ability to operationally define and measure both the criteria and contingencies of change; the sensitivity people talk of feelings as facts, and see in their comparative impreciseness and subjectivity an orientation that is more in keeping with the spirit and complexity of the human condition. And yet, for all their traditional and widely publicized differences, they are, at least from the perspective governing this chapter, in curious union as New Conservatives. Their phenotypic differences notwithstanding, they are genotypically more alike than they would care to admit.

For the behavior modifier, the happenings of the sixties reinforced the belief that massive social institutions were beyond change, that individuals engaged in trying to change them were continually punished, and that the positive net effects of the enterprise were both unobservable and probably statistically insignificant. Not only was the effort inconsequential, but also those involved in it emerged from the experience with a deep and painful sense of personal incompetence.

What the behavior modification movement promises its

adherents is the restoration of individual control and competence that the events of our recent past have torn away. To
be sure, it is a highly limited and questionable kind of control
and a very restricted sense of competence, but, in a social
order that has demonstrated its unwillingness to bend, small
gifts can neither be overlooked nor rejected with patrician-
like disdain. The only real difference between the behavior
modifier and the sensitivity enthusiast is the source from
which this new sense of control and competence is sought.
For the behavior modifier the source is still external to himself. Control, even in a limited form, can be derived by shaping the behavior of another human being, especially in a situation where the shaper, by virtue of his acknowledged
dominance, can vary the contingencies of reinforcement. Of
course, the manipulation is usually undertaken and understood to be in the client's interest, but that neither dimin-
ishes nor tarnishes the sense of being able to assert a level
of personal control over events that was not possible when
the client was the social order itself. And oh, the accompanying sense of competence and task completion! Unlike the situation with respect to problems in the area of social action or
even traditional psychotherapy, where change is infuriat-
ingly slow and uneven, results can now be achieved rather
quickly. One can see things begin, change, and end; one can,
in short, observe the fruit of one's labors in ways that were
heretofore only inferable, usually through some elaborate
pretense at extrapolation. Compared to the "schedule of reinforcement" under which the practice of social intervention
takes place, the practice of behavior modification offers its
practitioners immediate feedback and an almost instantaneous feeling of competence.

3. Magic, Mysticism, and Religion: Power from the Beyond

The reemergence of interest in new forms of religion and
in the arts of the occult highlights still another aspect of the
New Conservative attitude toward the world: the feeling
that one's own impotence is somehow either purposeful or
part of a much larger chain of events over which human con-

trol is both unwise and impossible. There is nothing new about the tendency, especially during periods of difficulty, to submit oneself to the presumed puppeteering of an external force. What is somewhat different about the current resignation is the equating of the "let it be" orientation with the receipt of an immediate reward, ecstacy, or sense of relatedness.

If people come to believe that the social order is inexorable and unresponsive to human intervention, it helps if one can develop a view of the cosmos that serves to cloak this unresponsiveness with a new meaning. It is doubly helpful if the cloak also enables its believers to deal with some of their own survival needs. Magic and mysticism serve these dual purposes rather well. To begin with, they provide a sense of instant continuity with the past. In addition, they offer "meditative sets" by which an "out of this world" reality can be used to either supplement or replace the limits imposed by the current social order. Religion, on the other hand, has always provided the social framework within which behavior becomes more ordered. The new religions, for all their apparent differences, provide either a sense of order or a new symbolism for dealing with the consequences of human dislocation and its accompanying impotence. Thus, whether we are talking about the followers of the Guru Maharaji, the Jesus freaks, or those who endlessly chant their Hari Krishnas on the sidewalks of our cities, we are talking about people for whom the problems of control can only be solved after one has accepted and celebrated the symbolic power of one's limitations.

4. The Primitivization of America: The Final Solution

In a very real sense, most of the opportunities for rationalized disengagement presented thus far do not demand the physical separation of the individual from the society he has found so frightening. One can, for example, continue to hold a job and still be a weekend encounter-group addict or an ardent follower and financial contributor to the Divine Light Mission's "Perfect Master." But when all else fails, when the temporary relief and limited control offered by the sensitivity movement, science, mysticism, or religion prove insufficient, a more radical option is required. This option, this final solution, involves the total withdrawal of the individual from the existing body politic and his ensuing commitment to the development of a completely separate and alternative intentional community.

Generally, the alternative communities created thus far by those who have chosen to absent themselves from the system seem to be oriented toward a form of primitivization. As if heeding Thoreau's call that we "simplify, simplify, simplify," the communes and collectives that are springing up are getting it together by returning to the soil, resurrecting the virtues of the organic farming process, or rediscovering the forgotten pleasures of macrame, pottery making and other forms of individual, and therefore presumably purer, craftsmanship. More often than not, these alternative communities are located in rural settings such as Big Island Creek Pipestem, West Virginia (Big Island Creek Folks), Summertown, Tennessee (The Farm), Naturita, Colorado (Magic Animal Farm), and Louisa, Virginia (Twin Oaks Community).

The importance of the movement to primitivize America lies less in debating the comparative virtues of any one of the intentional communities than in understanding the force of their appeal and the implications of their continued growth. To return to our basic theme, it is no accident that the resurgence of interest in the development of small, self-contained, earth-oriented intentional communities should follow so closely on the heels of the disasters of the sixties. Most of those who have succumbed to the lure of the land are young, white, and well-educated people, with good or potentially good incomes, the very ones who fell apart most as a consequence of the events of the recent past. For them, the primitivization of America, coupled with their seclusion in manageable settings, provides the only hope of recapturing the sense of personal control and competence that was lost dur-

ing the sixties. Yet, always mindful that their behavior can
be viewed as a colossal cop-out, they have been careful to
wrap their withdrawal in the rhetoric of the cultural revolution. As the people in the Magic Animal Farm (1974) put it:

> We wish to live with the earth rather than on it.
> Magic Animal Farm is not a retreat. We are not drop-
> outs, but consciously chose the relative isolation of
> Roc Creek to help us revamp our life styles on planes
> of time & space. We wind no clocks at Magic Animal
> Farm, but the seasons & their responsibilities arrive
> with a certainty that allows no procrastination. Our
> first priority is to learn how to take care of ourselves,
> each other & the earth in the time alloted to us
> (p. 45).

Or, as an advertisement for a book (*Free Ourselves* by Ar-
thur Aron, 1974) reads:

> In our movement for social change, we have in many
> ways, lost touch with our humanistic values—post-
> poning them till "after the revolution." Art believes
> that to realize our values we must *live* them by chang-
> ing ourselves and creating a giant personal/social/
> cultural alternative that will develop into the world we
> seek.... (p. 22).

The opportunities offered by the new communes and intentional alternatives are many and varied, ranging from intense group spirituality to experimentation with open mar-
riages and other nonpossessive forms of sharing to straight,
work-oriented collectivism and communal child rearing to
more individualized forms of "being" not very different from
the life-styles left behind. But the variety of contents notwithstanding, the movement's principal attraction lies in
what it promises its recruits: a restored sense of participation, the removal of anonymity, and the possibility of being
taken seriously and having an impact on shaping the structure of one's life-space. It offers, in short, an opportunity to

replace impotence, aloneness, and depression with total involvement in a setting that is purposefully created so as to remain manageable. Functional apoliticalization and physical withdrawal are certainly not too high a price to pay for the return of a significant degree of control over one's immediate existence. The fact that the primitivization process brings with it its own brand of revolutionary rhetoric is just so much frosting on the cake.

Traumatic events have a way of turning old friends into new adversaries. Many of today's New Conservatives were once visibly in the forefront of the struggle for a more equitable and humane society. Their involvement then was as great as their disengagement is today. They were the people of whom Eldridge Cleaver (1968) wrote:

> There is in America today a generation of white youth that is truly worthy of a black man's respect, and this is a rare event in the foul annals of American history. From the beginning of the contact between blacks and whites, there has been very little reason for a black man to respect a white, with such exceptions as John Brown and others lesser known. But respect commands itself and it can neither be given nor withheld when it is due. If a man like Malcolm X could change and repudiate racism, if I, myself, and other former Muslims can change, if young whites can change, then there is hope for America. It was certainly strange to find myself, while steeped in the doctrine that all whites were devils by nature, commanded by the heart to applaud and acknowledge respect for these young whites—despite the fact that they are descendants of the masters and I the descendant of slave. The sins of the fathers are visited upon the heads of the children —but only if the children continue in the evil deeds of the fathers (pp. 82–83).

Many of Cleaver's formerly eulogized "descendants of the masters" have retired from the fray, content, it seems, to pursue a much narrower, oftentimes more exotic, and certainly less dangerous form of personal liberation. Their defection is important not only in terms of the resources, talent, and spirit that have been lost, but also because it tells us something about the nature of how we experience and respond to trauma. In part, this chapter is an explanation of this phenomenon.

For some of the New Conservatives the trauma began long before they were born; for others it was an integral part of their emergence as human beings in twentieth-century America. And, as previously indicated, it is difficult to predict how long the attitude of New Conservativism will dominate the actions and choices of people. But what seems to be clear, at least from our own point of view, is that social disengagement, however rationalized or imbued with transcendent legitimacy, can only serve to perpetuate the "evil deeds of the fathers"—and in perpetuating those deeds, we perpetuate our own inability to finally, fully, and fundamentally regain a significant measure of control over our lives.

6

Toward a Conception of Human Possibilities

Each age writes its own epitaph—indeed, creates its own eternity—with respect to how it conceives of man and how it conceives of change. We, either as heirs or as participants in this timeless process, must assume the responsibility for defending, changing, or destroying that which we have inherited or wish to bequeath to others (Goldenberg, 1969). It would not be unfair to state that in the final analysis humankind defines itself through the societies it chooses to allow to be born and to live, and those it decides must be killed.

The problems of social intervention, no differently from those associated with the creation of totally new societies or settings, are problems which can be understood in terms of the particular conception of man one elects to infuse with both meaning and validity. The societies that we create, the means we choose to create them, and the ways we go about changing them are all concrete instances of how different conceptions about man and about human possibilities determine the form and content of the societies we build, perpetuate, alter, or terminate.

The infusion of meaning and validity into a particular conception of man is not a scientific act. Neither does it have anything to do with a purposefully dispassionate pursuit of truth, regardless of how elaborate the incantations are that accompany it. When, for example, Skinner (1971) tells us that "a scientific analysis of behavior dispossesses autonomous man and turns control he has been said to exert over to the environment," he is not making a scientific statement any more than he is providing us with an accurate overview of history. Similarly, when our humanist friends lash out at "Leibnitz's monads," seek to canonize the subjective aspects of our nature, or warn us, as Polanyi (1962) has, that "one may disassemble a watch and examine all of its parts (and reassemble them) without learning anything about the meaningful function of the watch or about the nature of time," they are being neither scientific nor philosophical.

Statements about the nature of man are as much political statements as they are attempts to decipher the hidden symbols and meanings of our collective soul. Their function is to provide the rationales, establish the expectations, and encourage the development of those social structures through which self-fulfilling prophesies are actualized (Bugental, 1967). The importance, for example, of what Waters (1948) has called "mechanomorphic" views of man (views of man which hold that the human being is essentially a reactive processing apparatus driven by built-in instincts, physiological drives, and imprinted habits) is the legitimacy they lend to those, like Skinner, for whom a society essentially led and managed by elitists represents both the ultimate form of civilized living and the highest expression of social purpose. In short, whether man is dethroned or ennobled with respect to his centrality in the universe is as much a political problem as it is an issue of philosophical contention.

The social interventionist, no differently from anyone else, cannot be viewed as acting in a socio-political-historical vacuum. The processes and goals of social intervention take on their meaning as much from the future as from the past. The importance of what has been called a conception of humankind is that it provides a semblance of continuity to the social interventionist enterprise. Its function is to make action both intelligible and meaningful beyond the exigencies of the immediate situation.

Universal Needs

The purpose of this final chapter is to share with the reader some preliminary thoughts concerning the development of a guiding conception of human possibilities. Unfortunately, the problem with most such attempts is that they lend themselves to the propagation of "universal need theories," theories based on the hierarchical ordering of needs and their sequential fulfillment over time. Maslow's (1954) "holistic-dynamic" approach to personality, for example, is one such theory in that it posits an "unfolding process" in which "lower-order needs" (physiological and safety needs) must be satisfied before the "higher needs" (self-actualization and aesthetic needs) become either prepotent or assume a position of greater urgency in the motivational hierarchy that distinguishes the human condition.

These universal needs are not presented here as a theory which seeks to account for the general development of personality. Rather, the term universal needs is used to connote the conditions toward which the human organism strives or is inclined independent of age, level of sophistication, or stage of development. The unfolding process, therefore, is not defined as a sequential process whose beginning and end are tied to different drives or symbolized by qualitatively different kinds of satisfactions. Quite to the contrary, *the human condition is its possibilities,* and these possibilities, or universal needs, set humankind apart from all other forms of existense, and the experience of these possibilities is the essential and unchanging mandate of our mode of being in the world.

1. The Need for a Sense of Self

The first of the conditions toward which the human organism strives is that state of personal awareness or identity often referred to as one's self-concept. From our perspective, we would call it the need for a viable *sense of self*. And by the term "self" we are referring to the experience through which one comes to view one's being as separate and distinct from all others' while at the same time intimately related to a particular group of one's fellow beings. It is the sense of a unique and nonreplicable personal identity and history, but one that is simultaneously bound up in a broader social awareness and racial and ethnic consciousness. In its final expression, it is the process through which one seeks answers to the questions "Who am I?, Where do I come from?, and Where will I finally rest?"

In a fundamental way the need for a sense of self is oriented toward the reconstruction of one's past, toward the discovery of one's racial, sexual, and ethnic prehistory, and toward recapturing the roots of one's group heritage. It is certainly no accident, therefore, that most attempts to subjugate a people begin by trying to deny their collective sense of identity and historical relationships. The tattooing of numbers on the arms of the inmates of Buchenwald, Treblinka, and the rest of Hitler's death camps had less to do with the bureaucratic need for efficient bookkeeping that it did with the desire to obliterate a people's ethnic consciousness. In our country, the success of slavery as a social and economic institution was predicated on the destruction of the black person's cultural frame of reference and the sense of historical perspective that invariably accompanies it. When Malcolm Little became Malcolm X he was terminating and denying his oppressors the right to continue to create his pseudo-identity. When Cassius Marcellus Clay became Muhammad Ali he was substituting his analysis of his racial ties for the "antianalysis" that had preceded it. When females "become" their husbands' second names they are made to do so for reasons far more complicated than social registration and simplified taxation.

The concept of America as a melting pot of different peoples, traditions, customs, and perspectives is only the latest and perhaps most sophisticated mechanism by which the group-specific aspects of the sense of self have been undermined by the prevailing social order. The term melting pot has traditionally been used to connote the creation of a totally new entity or substance out of the residues of whatever ingredients originally went into the pot. In practice, of course, this has neither been the case nor the intention. When Jews sought acceptance by assimilation into the American social order by changing or Americanizing their names, they were under no delusions that *everyone* was engaged in a similar renaming. It was always clear that one was trying to mask one's ethnic heritage, not contribute to the development of a new and evolving national identity. The promulgation of the myth of America as a melting pot had both functional and utilitarian purposes. It helped create the conditions under which historical group roots could be undermined, or at least manipulated, to the service of those who controlled the existing social, economic, and political levers of the society. As Glazer and Moynihan (1963) point out, "the notion that the intense and unprecedented mixture of ethnic and religious groups in American life was soon to blend into a homogeneous end product has outlived its usefulness, and also its credibility," is but another way of affirming the reality of its nefarious intents.

The need for a viable sense of self, while initially retrospective in focus, has clear and undeniable consequences in reality. It organizes the world and its often ambiguous signals in ways that relate directly to oneself both as a distinct individual and as a member of a larger group that shares a perspective from which events and intentions can be interpreted. As such, it provides the individual with a reaffirmable context within which actions assume a meaning beyond the moment of impact. It is the irreducible reference point or ground from which movement springs. It is, in short, the fulcrum on which one's basic integrity is defined and made nonnegotiable.

2. The Need for a Sense of Personal Impact

If the need for a sense of self is retrospective in nature, the need for a sense of personal impact is fully directed toward the dynamics of the present. When we speak of the need for a sense of personal impact, we mean the experience of participating directly, fully, and with few preconditions in the process by which the boundaries of one's freedom are determined. It is, however, more than that. It is the sense that one can and does have a recognizable and continually reaffirmed input on the decisions that ultimately affect the quality of one's life. Finally, it is the sense that there is a reality and credibility to one's personal involvement, and that the questioning and changing of one's social, economic, and political world is a sacred trust and not a precarious privilege bestowed by others and eternally subject to revocation.

The universal need to experience a sense of control over the conditions under which one lives is what is meant by the term self-determination. It connotes a mode of being in which one's actions in the world define the meaning of one's humanity. To be self-determining is to be proactive, restless, and intensely committed to that which is creative and ennobling of the human enterprise. It is the stance one assumes in the face of increased pressures toward passivity, conformity, and complacency.

The need for a sense of personal impact—of participating directly in the process of determining one's fate—is a concept that flies directly in the face of those for whom the social order is perceived as a means of managing others. It is a dangerous concept insofar as it delegitimizes the virtue of elitist leadership. The phrase "maximum feasible participation," for example, may one day stand alongside the wording of the Supreme Court's 1954 desegregation decision ("with all deliberate speed") as one of the more controversial if not clearly conceptualized sentences in recent American history. Its effect, perhaps inadvertently, was not only to redefine the relationship between helping programs and the recipients but also to create the conditions for a potential shift in political power and social control. What may very well have begun as a well-intentioned but relatively minor attempt to involve the poor in the planning and implementation of opportunity programs may one day be looked upon as the most significant by-product of the War on Poverty, and, of course, an important reason for the termination. In essence, the concept of maximum feasible participation confronted political systems with the need to share, and perhaps even relinquish, a good deal of the power they had so studiously and cautiously reserved for themselves. On the other hand, by making it more legitimate for the heretofore completely powerless to determine the course of their own lives and development, the wording of the Economic Opportunity Act of 1964 opened a Pandora's box of problems and conflicts, some of which may yet change the existing social fabric of our society in some unanticipated ways.

The point, of course, is that the need for a sense of personal impact, far from being contained or curtailed by sudden openings in the system, is an insatiable and contagious offspring of the human spirit. Thus, when Schlesinger (1965) says that "revolutions accelerate not from despair but from hope," he is simply reaffirming the notions that, conditions notwithstanding, the innate tendency of the human organism is to welcome rather than recoil from the possibilities of personal involvement in the decisions around which one's life and times become ordered.

3. The Need for a Sense of Transcendence

Lastly, there is what we might call the need for a *sense of transcendence,* the need for opportunities through which it becomes possible to relate one's life and times to the unrelenting, almost mystical pull of history. As finite beings caught somewhere in the midpassage of civilization, we are a part of an evolutionary process whose beginning and end will never be a part of our direct experience. We were neither present at our inception as a species, nor will we in all likelihood be in attendance at our collective demise. Nevertheless, as conscious and self-reflective beings we seek meaning, a process through which we come into contact with the implications of our existential passage, a process whose elusive goal is the creation of a personal and collective perspective in a constantly changing matrix characterized by all the temporariness and transience of a super- or postindustrialized society. As human beings we seek to go beyond our immediate experiences; we strive to approach the implicit meaning of things, and we seek to understand our travails. This, after all, is the ultimate and splendid fiction that allows us to exalt the human condition above all other forms of being.

The need for a sense of transcendence is what binds us, simultaneously, to the future and the past. It is also the vehicle by which we go beyond ourselves and the groups from which we derive our initial heritage or toward which we gravitate. It is what Alinsky (1971) meant when he wrote:

> A major revolution to be won in the immediate future is the dissipation of man's illusion that his own welfare can be separate from that of all others (p. 23).

To transcend oneself and one's group is to reach out for the fabric that joins people together, to pursue the human chorus whose song will never be captured or contained.

To be human is to exist in the past, in the present, and in the future—all at the same time, and to derive from each temporal plane a measure of intensity needed to infuse one's journey with new energy and meaning (see Figure 1). From the past we draw our individual and collective roots; in the present we seek to reshape our destinies; the future binds us to each other in ways that go beyond our imaginings. A part of us will always be private and unalterably nonreplicable;

Figure 1.   A Conception of the Human Condition

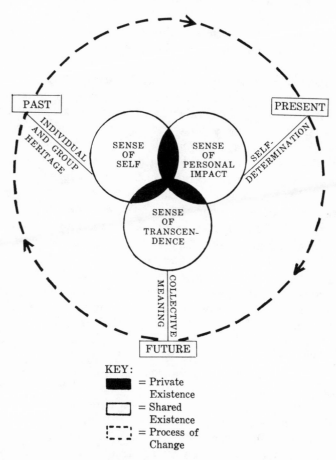

KEY:
= Private Existence
= Shared Existence
= Process of Change

a part of us will be public, shared, and open to review; and our existence as a whole will forever be a part of an unseen, unknown process of change.

In the final analysis, the essential meaning of the human condition rests with these possibilities. Its clarity as well as its ambiguity, its heroism as well as its denigration, will always be a part of that condition. Such is the destiny of an organism condemned to self-reflection. We cannot choose to be human—we can only choose to be humane.

A Final Note: The University and the Problems of Oppression and Social Intervention

Most of us lead what can only be termed uncomfortable if not totally contradictory lives. For myself, the writing of this book, initially undertaken with a certain zest and flamboyance, soon became a relatively joyless and painful experience. The reasons are now as clear as they are undiminishing: in trying to provide others with an analysis of oppression and the problems of social intervention one is forced, perhaps as never before, to use oneself and one's setting as a primary source of data for understanding the contradictions one is writing about. For myself, this has meant looking anew at the formal social institution, the university, of which I have been more or less a part for most of my working years.

The university, no differently from any other setting entrusted with the task of processing (i.e., socializing and legitimizing) people into a society oriented to goods and power, consists of a complex series of interlocking, though by no means mutual, interests defined over time and invested with a degree of apparent, if not actual, validity. Its composition bespeaks a delicate balance of power groups, institutional relationships, and spheres of influence. Each segment may bring with it some slightly altered view of the world, but together they define the university as a community, give it uniqueness, shape its pattern of enduring values and traditions, and share in its perpetuation. In short, when all is said and done, the university defines a way of life and sets the limits, both political and intellectual, of acceptable and unacceptable deviance (Goldenberg, 1974). It does so through its definition of "scholarly research," its relationship to the broader society, its departmental decisions concerning tenure, the model of interpersonal relations it makes available to its staff, students, and faculty, or the manner in which it deals with the most political of supposedly nonpolitical issues, academic freedom. This definition and the limits that invariably accompany it are not discernibly different or in opposition to those that prevail in the rest of society. The university is, indeed, the handmaiden of the social and political order from which it derives its resources.

There is little doubt that the university, like its companion social institutions, has often succeeded in cloaking its motives with rhetoric that is as confusing as it is impressive. It can, for example, speak out, usually quite eloquently, about the need to change, "rekindle our faith in the capacity of people to choose wisely for themselves within a climate of honest search," and recommit itself to dealing with the harsh moral and political realities of an imperfect society. This done, it can then conclude, quite alone, that it is mankind's "institution dedicated to the search for truth and the value of intellectual inquiry" (Harvard, 1971). And then, almost as if believing that the power of such rhetoric brings with it an awesome imperial blessing, it continues its financial investments in blatantly racist and oppressive governments and oversees its own domestic sprawl over the communities in which it sits.

Every myth and contradiction we have pointed to in our analysis of the American experience is mirrored, albeit in different form, within the university. The notion, for example, that the university provides a unique and supportive context for assumptions and questioning is certainly open to doubt. It is no accident that much of the formative work of Darwin, Marx, Freud, and Einstein, the four theoreticians generally acknowledged to have had the greatest impact on our thinking about the human condition in the last 100 years, should have been conducted outside the walls of academia. Rather, it appears as if the university, far from encouraging creativity, is more at home in its role of refining, replicating, and processing *existing* modes of thought. Similarly, the rhetoric of academic freedom, pluralism, and independent scholarship can be viewed as convenient subterfuges for the perpetuation of private entrepreneurship that is in keeping with the underlying ethos of a society predicated on individual competition and exploitation. Finally, there is the university's myth about science and the apolitical nature of the heralded quest for truth.

In fact, there is nothing apolitical about our research and the ways we conduct it, certainly not in the social sciences. Methodologies and methodological controversies aside, our research is always purposeful and political. Let me offer one small example. For many years I have been involved in the problems of understanding juvenile delinquency and in designing and implementing programs of help. While writing this book I reviewed some of the research in the area to see the extent to which such research was restricted to studies of the delinquent as opposed to others within the juvenile justice system whose actions and behaviors could be presumed to have an impact on the problem. Over the last ten years, as reported in the *Psychological Abstracts*, there have been 162 separate, university-based studies of the juvenile delinquent. Virtually all of the studies, independent of methodology, theoretical orientation, or accompanying rationale, found conclusive proof of the delinquent's underlying psychopathology. Depending on the conceptual framework of the researcher, the delinquent was either schizophrenic, had a poor self-image, could not put off immediate gratification, had little ego strength, or suffered from a social learning deficit. Over the same ten-year period only two studies sought to inquire into the underlying pathology of the police who arrested the adolescents, the judges before whom the alleged delinquents were brought and who eventually sentenced them, or the keepers into whose hands they were finally delivered.

Is this science? Or is this but another example of how the scientific enterprise is used to focus attention on the simplest and least socially threatening aspect of a problem? Money is available, especially from the federal government, for academicians to study the offender; but resources are hard to come by when the subject of inquiry shifts from the offender to the system he has supposedly offended. Academicians, especially those for whom the "publish or perish" lifestyle has become synonymous with self-worth, professional advancement, and acceptance into the scientific community, are not likely to be overly critical about the source of their support, the focus of their research, or the political implications and potential uses of their findings.

But it is no accident that most of us who inhabit the university should be so out of touch with the contradictions of which we are a part. We have been conditioned, for example, to define science as the attempt to study and understand the human condition, *not to change it*. We too have been processed for an existence that is implicitly self-serving if not obviously supportive of the entire existing social order. But we perpetuate that social order, not only in terms of our research and studied disengagement, but also through the credentialing process we have created, and now use with blind allegiance to mold those who will follow or replace us. A former student recently sent me some of his "comic" writing, reflections on his graudate school experiences. Let the reader, especially the graduate student, judge its accuracy.

JUST FINISHED GRADUATE SCHOOL

A: I just finished graduate school!
B: You just finished graduate school?
A: Yeah, I just finished graduate school.
B: Terrific! How long did it take you?
A: Seven years.
B: Seven years! That's not very good is it?
A: It's very good.
B: What do you mean, very good?
A: It's *very* good!
B: Isn't that kind of long?
A: Yeah, it's long.
B: But that's not good.
A: Sure it's good. The longer the better.
B: What do you mean "the longer the better?" That's crazy.

A: I mean *the longer the better*. Everyone knows the most courageous people hold out the longest.

B: Hold out against what?

A: The brainwashing!

The first year I was there they sat us in a room and lectured us incessantly. They made us read propaganda. They even made us criticize one another so we'd think right. They tried to get information out of us. But they couldn't get it out of me. I just gave them name, rank, and serial number.

It was frightening! I saw my friends, too, one by one. My friends, once they'd been real people, who laughed and cried. Now they were mere robots, echoing the latest change in the party line.

They tortured me! They sat me down and shined a light in my eyes. "Where's your interest in research?" they said. But I wouldn't talk. They couldn't get *that* out of me! Finally after seven years, I had passed the point of pain. I felt that I had held out long enough.

I confessed and they gave me my Ph.D.

ARCHAEOLOGISTS DIG PSYCHOLOGISTS

A thousand years from now archaeologists dig and find evidence "psychologists" had been there. They dig up tools—it turns out tools, research tools, were very important to these people, and try to piece together the life patterns of these people.

They found two kinds of tools suggesting there were two different groups of psychologists. There were those who used "hard" tools and those who used "soft" tools.

The ones who used "hard" tools lived by trapping for small game. They set their traps (called "experiments" or "laboratories") and at the end of the day would go to see what they had caught in their traps. They'd find rats, rabbits, or pigeons, and sometimes parts of larger animals—a human eye or brain, a foot, an ear—but never larger animals intact.

Those with the soft tools used "nets." They caught larger animals in the nets, even *groups* of larger animals, but they could never hold them. The animals always got away.

In order to become a member of the tribe one had to make his own tool, a very arduous and painstaking process, which was called "graduate school." It was important to make a tool that looked different from anyone else's tool. If it looked too much like someone else's tool it was considered cause for shame. There was an exception. If one's tool looked like the tools made in the shop of the old toolmaker that one worked with, it was not considered a cause for shame, but a sign of respect.

Once one had made one's tool, and was accepted into the tribe there seemed to be some different patterns. Mysteriously, some buried their tools ten feet under the ground, left the tribe, and were never heard from again. Others sat and polished their tools for the rest of their life.

Moral: The freedom of academic freedom is largely academic.

Philip Rosenthal
Spring, 1974

Those of us who choose to remain a part of the university, especially those of us who profess a continuing involvement in the problems of oppression and social intervention, can no longer do so under the delusion that we are somehow a part of a less malignant or more enlightened outpost of the social order. We, no less than our compatriots in the police departments, welfare agencies, courts, and in all the other formal social institutions that regulate the passage of souls through the turnstiles of our society, are, indeed, the enemy, and we will remain so for as long as our actions lend credibility to a social order whose underlying ethos is destructive of the human possibility. It is this that Otto Rene Castillo was telling us in his poem *Apolitical Intellectuals*.

One day
    the apolitical
    intellectuals
    of my country
    will be interrogated
    by the simplest
    of our people.

They will be asked
    what they did
    when their nation died out
    slowly,
    like a sweet fire,
    small and alone.

No one will ask them
    about their dress,
    their long siestas
    after lunch,
    No one will want to know
    about their sterile combats
    with "the idea
    of the nothing."

No one will care about
    their higher financial learning.
They won't be questioned
    on Greek mythology,
    or regarding their self-disgust
    when someone within them
    begins to die
    the coward's death.

They'll be asked nothing
    about their absurd
    justifications,
    born in the shadow
    of the total lie.

On that day,
   the simple men will come.

Those who had no place
   in the books and poems
   of the apolitical intellectuals,
   but daily delivered
   their bread and milk,
   their tortillas and eggs,
   those who mended their clothes.
   those who drove their cars,
   who cared for their dogs and gardens
   and worked for them, and they'll ask:

"What did you do when the poor
   suffered, when tenderness
   and life
   burned out in them?"

Apolitical intellectuals
   of my sweet country
   you will not be able to answer.

A vulture of silence
   will eat your gut.

Your own misery
   will pick at your soul

And you will be mute in your shame.

EPILOGUE

They are gone now; one to oblivion, the other to the abyss. The years have triumphed, much like the sea, always pounding and finally muting the once joyous rocks. Your anger has been quieted, your visions numbed, your struggles largely unrecorded.

But for some—for one in particular—even the fiercest of seas will never betray the glory that accompanied your tears. Goodbye Frima and Nuta Goldenberg. All that remains is the memory of your passion. Perhaps that will prove to be enough.

NOTES

Chapter 1

1. This should not be interpreted to mean that *all* delinquent or deviant behavior on the part of adolescents is necessarily a response to conditions of oppression. What we have sought to describe is an altered context within which it is no longer either necessary or valid to routinely apply the label of pathology to any and all behavior that violates existing social "norms."

2. With regard to this point, it is interesting to note that there are more rules governing the behavior of students in some high schools than there are for convicts in penitentiaries.

3. The ultimate expression of personal abuse is, of course, suicide. Suicide rates among the young, the poor, and minority groups, particularly the American Indian, are clearly in excess of the national norm.

4. It should be clear that much of the conceptual and theoretical justification for this view was provided by the so-called liberal social-scientific establishment. From the now very familiar sociological concept of the "culture of poverty" (Moynihan, 1965), to the more psychologically oriented rationales stressing such variables as "poor self-image," "deficient motivation," and "inadequate impulse control" (Iverson, 1965), the set was created whereby the problems of poverty could be viewed, rather comfortably we might add, as instances of individual and group malfunctioning.

5. We might also point out our belief that the few instances in which federally funded community action programs actually began to deal with the institutional sources of poverty, educational systems, employer and labor union practices, and so on, had more to do with the ultimate castration of the War on Poverty than any of the more publicized reasons and rationales emanating from Washington (e.g., fiscal insobriety, inadequate research, poor cost-benefit-effectiveness ratios, etc.).

6. In all fairness to Argyris, it should be pointed out that in retrospect he, too, termed his work with the State Department as unsuccessful. It is hard, however, to know what he would define as a successful intervention in light of his insistence that his methods are value-free. In this context, it appears that value-free means that Argyris is unconcerned with questions as to whether or not his work is used to help the State Department oppress others. If his work had been successful, presumably, the department would be more efficient in its oppression. The problem is, indeed, one of values and the decision involves relationships between these values and whom one wishes to work with in furthering an organization's objectives.

7. It is interesting to note, for example, the degree to which liberal support in terms of money and prestige was withdrawn from the civil rights movement when black groups made clear their intention to run their own show by accepting white financial support but not continuing to heed the advice or direction of their contributors.

Chapter 3

1. We might briefly mention that in most societies laws operate to monitor the manner in which particular values are expressed. Religions function to either reinforce existing values or to provide noncompetitive alternatives, and the mental health professions serve to treat what is considered deviant within, or a significant deviation from, the chosen values. In other words, judgments concerning the ethics, morality, and well-being of citizens follow from, rather than precede, the particular values that a society deems central to its existence. Consequently, pluralism, certainly in its pure form, is generally a meaningless abstraction.

2. It would be counterproductive to enter into extended discussions now as to whether or not the attainment of goods and power *should* be at the heart of our society's value system. We shall talk about what *could* or *might be* later in the book. For the present, it is best that we heed Alinsky and Sanders' (1970) admonition to stay within the bounds of what we have experienced most directly and consistently. For the vast majority of us, the garnering of goods and power has in one way or another been the cornerstone of what we have been taught to view as "good" and have accepted with more than a little passion.

3. It is always very difficult to deal, however briefly, with the relationship between intellectual and/or religious thought and the development of an exploitative system without making reference to Tawney's (1926) seminal work in this area. The reader is urged to review this work.

4. We shall, however, return to this problem later in the book, for it does matter, from a very practical social interventionist perspective, how and in what order questions of class, race, and sex enter into one's analysis of a particular situation. For the present, all we wish to make clear is that the assumptions underlying the system virtually demand the promulgation of victims. It is a situation analogous to the one described by Sartre (1948) in his analysis of the anti-Semite's need to create his Jew.

5. It should be clear that we are employing the notion of a "journey" in a purely metaphorical sense for purposes of illustration. In reality, we know that for most disadvantaged people the journey is undermined so early in life as to never really begin. The combined effects of inherited poverty and the initial struggle for survival are usually enough to undo any lingering hopes of ever becoming a part of the game one has been conditioned to revere. The debilitating nature of these early exercises are amply documented in the work of Cloward and Elman (1966), Strauss (1967), and Valentine (1968).

6. Much of the current unrest in the mental health professions centers around the perception of psychotherapy as an "adjustment-oriented" instrument designed and used to both defuse legitimate anger and further becloud the economic, racial, and sexual issues that underlie much of the psychological suffering in our society. Not surprisingly, the slogan of this unrest is "Therapy Means Change, Not Adjustment." For the reader interested in exploring this issue further, the work of Agel (1973) and Clark and Jaffe (1973) provide appropriate points of departure.

7. It is interesting to note just how often and closely the kinds of problems we, the mental health professionals, become engaged in coincide with the flow of funds from Washington. During the now much-romanticized days of the War on Poverty, when money from OEO was both available and "coming down the pike" in substantial amounts, one found the helping professions deeply enmeshed in the problems associated with being poor. Now, when the rhetoric of law and order, closely followed by Nixon's Public Enemy

Number 1, the drug problem, has become the dominant ideological theme pervading most programs originating from Washington, we find the mental health establishment becoming increasingly concerned with the problems associated with crime and addiction. The "fit" is too close to be either accidental or unimportant.

8. We shall have much more to say later in this chapter and in the one that follows by way of contrasting the meaning and significance of the "involuntary alienation" available to the poor and the powerless and the type of "voluntary alienation" that is at the heart of much of the activity currently called "countercultural." For the present, however, all we want to make clear is that there is a vast difference, both in quality and purpose, between the alienation of poor people and nonwhites, the traditionally expendable, and the self-imposed and oftentimes romanticized searches of middle- and upper-class white youth who voluntarily opt out of the system in search of "deeper meanings" and alternative life-styles.

9. A debt is owed to Lee Regal (1974) for pointing out the fallacy of assuming that goods and power are isomorphically related to each other in every individual case. Her analysis of the situation confronting those considered to be a part of the middle classes is one which focuses attention on the consequences of possessing greater amounts of goods but not the actual power one might assume would invariably be a part of the situation of increased material resources. For her, the issues associated with power are somewhat different from those associated with goods, although both are assumed to be important with respect to understanding nonrelations.

10. Again, we wish to make clear that we view the volitional opting-out behavior of the affluent as different, both in form and content, from what we have called the involuntary alienation of the poor and powerless. Voluntary alienation is characterized by the existence of at least three conditions that do not apply to the traditionally excluded. First, it is a *real choice* in the sense that it represents a qualitatively different form of material existence; second, it is always predicated on a *rejection* of the existing value system; and third, it is usually *reversible*. If things get too tough the individual can always return to a materially, if not psychologically, comfortable level of existence.

Chapter 4

1. In a recent paper dealing with the problems of social service reform, Ron Edmonds (1974) has attempted to spell out some of the conditions under which it becomes possible for people occupying different levels of social and economic power to form cooperative relationships. His analysis, based on what he terms "community minimums" and "institutional maximums," provides a framework for the development of intergroup coalitions. Nevertheless, the basis for this coalition rests explicitly on an awareness of and appreciation for the fact that the haves and have-nots in the social order initially begin to cooperate because of different group-specific needs rather than because of any innate awareness of their common plight.

2. The relatively recent realization that the problem of runaways, heretofore viewed as a lower-class phenomenon because it often involved young people leaving the home in order to pursue greater economic opportunity, has become a middle-class phenomenon. It is but the most obvious example of the rejection of the lifestyle of affluent, adult America (Libertoff, 1974). For, as it turns out, many middle-class adolescents are leaving home with the explicit purpose of *divesting* themselves of economic security. The panhandling and begging of once-affluent youth, the new street people, is a rather obvious attempt at downward class reversal and, of course, one of the reasons they get so little support from the "honestly" poor.

3. One ought not to take too lightly the appeal of the recent television series called *The American Family*. The public fascination with the Loud family had less to do with any one of the many dramatic issues portrayed (divorce, homosexuality, etc.) than it did with the simple and stark manner in which the decaying emptiness of a "successful" family was played out before a middle-American public already silently in tune with the Louds.

4. It is clearly easier to be specific about the goals of social intervention for poor people than for affluent people. It would be easy if social intervention with the affluent could be defined as the obverse of social intervention with the poor. In other words, if the goal of social intervention with the poor is to *get* goods and power, then the goal of social intervention with the affluent ought to be

to *give up* goods and power. Unfortunately, the simplicity and logic of this formulation may not be realistic given the nature and content of the American experience. It is certainly not realistic if one assumes a short time perspective on the problems of change in a superindustrialized technocracy. It may, however, be appropriate to view social intervention with the affluent as involving the process by which people develop the rationale for ultimately abandoning their surplus goods and power in the face of an organized and increasingly demanding class of historically disenfranchised people (Uhlig, 1974).

5. It should be clear, however, that in recent years the acceptance of class-crossing social interventionists has undergone significant change. No longer can the interventionist who crosses classes count on being embraced or given significant leadership responsibilities by the group with which he wishes to become affiliated. Rather, two trends are developing. First, social interventionists, their credibility and skills notwithstanding, are increasingly being urged to "work in your own backyard, get your own house in order"; and second, in those instances where the social interventionist is accepted, it is with the understanding that he serve at the pleasure of the group and he be expected to provide specific help, usually of a technical nature, upon request. In part, therefore, the overall degree of class-crossing is decreasing as a consequence of the increased tendency of groups to define themselves more rigidly along racial, sexual, ethnic, or class lines.

6. Alinsky became acutely aware of this problem and of his own needs in such situations. His work, particularly during the last years of his life, shifted more and more toward the questions involved in training others in the "art" of intervention. Also, with respect to the issues of leadership, his remark that "Periodic mass euphoria around a charismatic leader is not an organization; it's just the initial stage of agitation" bears serious consideration.

7. Each group, of course, maintains that *its* liberation will lead to the liberation of the others. Women believe that their emancipation will lead to the emancipation of males; the poor believe that their liberation will facilitate the liberation of the affluent; and people of the Third World that their freedom will result in the emancipation of their white oppressors. In each instance, rather than relinquishing the preciousness of a coherent group-specific analysis, the assumption is made that liberation is a phenomenon

that can be generalized automatically, that those excluded by a particular group's agenda will be freed when that agenda is realized. The statement that "What's good for General Motors is good for America" does, indeed, have its analog among the different oppressed groups in our society.

Chapter 5

1. It is interesting to note just how similar the New Conservatives are to what might be called the Old Liberals. For all their differences in rhetoric and life-style, they are united by what appears to be a common revulsion over the prospects of dealing directly with the vicissitudes of personal action in the world. For example, unlike the New Conservatives, the Old Liberals look at the world and continue to see rationality just round the corner. But like their younger compatriots, they are eternally optimistic about the progress and potential of mankind, and so long as that progress and potential demands taking no personal risks on their part they are in the forefront of every battle for human dignity and freedom. Theirs is a life-style of involvement in which struggles are forever occurring out there in a depersonalized world which could easily be transformed if only the forces of oppression (good people all) could be tempted to listen to the muted cries of the disenfranchised and disaffiliated. But the Old Liberals will not put themselves out there, for they have felt the horror that awaits those who have accepted the responsibility of first being what they want others to become. And so, the Old Liberals always seek to fulfill their visions and needs by continually creating two separate worlds for themselves. The first is a world of ongoing concern for a generalized and often abstract mankind, a concern bordering on genuine passion for both the oppressed and the oppressors. The second, however, is a world so constructed as to prevent themselves from ever having to change or give anything up, a world in which they do not risk exposing themselves or their own interests to the society from which they are demanding a commitment to self-reflection and self-renewal. It is in this sense that the Old Liberals are truly the parents of the New Conservatives.

2. In an excellent book entitled *The Con III Controversy: The Critics Look at the Greening of America,* Nobile (1971) has attempted to survey and interpret the varying reactions to Reich's epistle. Although Nobile's book was not, as he correctly points out,

"manipulated to provide a majority against the book," Nobile's own dedication best sums up our feelings about Reich's contribution. The dedication reads, very simply:

> "For Philip Berrigan #70173
> and
> Daniel Berrigan #23742-145
> who are greening in the
> Federal Correctional
> Institution at Danbury,
> Connecticut."

3. We are acutely aware that our description of the temper of the fifties and sixties is little more than an attempt to employ a perverse historical shorthand in depicting the feeling tone of a limited number of years. No single description of an age—much less of a decade—can accurately reflect the upheavals and dislocations of human thought and action that took place during that span of time. It is, therefore, of necessity, a description that is somewhat arbitrary, unreal, and incomplete. None of these decades existed in and of themselves, without continuity or overlap.

4. When we speak of the sensitivity movement we are referring to the conglomerate of group process and group dynamics practices that are employed to both define and treat problems as if they were solely or primarily of personal and interpersonal origins. Thus, we include in the movement such apparently diverse approaches and interests as those represented by the organizational developers on the one hand (Argyris, 1965) and the group-groping Esalen addicts on the other (Schutz, 1967). For all their differences, they are united by the belief that the problems of change and control must be confined to the individual and the small group. It should be clear, however, that the use of group dynamics need not be restricted to facilitating individual adjustment or creative withdrawal. The work of Singer, Whiton, and Fried (1970) is a good example of the use of group process methodology as a means of addressing harsh community realities.

REFERENCES

Chapter 1

Argyris, C. How effective is the State Department? *Yale Alumni Magazine*, May 1967, pp. 38–41.

Benedict, R. Continuities and discontinuities in cultural conditioning. In P. Mullahy (ed.) *A study of interpersonal relations.* New York: Hermitage Press, 1949.

Brown, C. *Manchild in the promised land.* New York: Macmillan, 1965.

Chorover, S. Big brother and psycho-technology. *Psychology Today,* October 1973.

Clark, K. B. *Dark ghetto: Dilemmas of social power.* New York: Harper & Row, 1965.

Cloward, R. A. *Power, poverty, and the involvement of the poor.* Testimony before the Senate Select Subcommittee on Poverty, Washington, D.C., June 29, 1965.

Community Research Review Committee of the Black United Front. *Review of the Laue project entitled Community Crisis Intervention.* Boston: May 1971.

Conners, C. K. Recent drug studies with hyperkinetic children. *Journal of Learning Disabilities,* 1971, *4* (9).

DiMascio, A., & Shader, R. *Psychotropic drugs—side effects.* Baltimore: Williams & Wilkins, 1970.

Friedenberg, E. Z. *The coming of age in America.* New York: Random House, 1963.

Goldenberg, I. I. *Build me a mountain: Youth, poverty, and the creation of new settings.* Cambridge: The M.I.T. Press, 1971.

Goldenberg, I. I. *The problem of safety in our inner-city schools: A view from the bottom.* In C. D. Perkins (Chairman), Hearings on H.R. 2650 before the General Subcommittee on Education, Washington, D.C., February 26, 1973.

Goldenberg, I. I., Keating, E. Businessmen and therapists: Prejudices against employment. In L. Simmons & M. Gold (eds.), *Discrimination and the addict*. Beverly Hills, Calif.: Sage Publications, 1973.

Goodman, P. *Growing up absurd*. New York: Macmillan, 1960.

Gordon, J. The disadvantaged boy: Implications for counseling. In A. Amos (ed.), *Counseling culturally disadvantaged youth*. Englewood Cliffs, N.J.: Prentice-Hall, 1967.

Grier, W. H., & Cobbs, P. M. *Black rage*. New York: Basic Books, 1968.

Hess, R. D., & Goldblatt, I. The status of adolescents in American society: A problem in social identity. *Child Development*, 1957, *28*, pp. 459–68.

Iverson, W. H. *The use of the non-professional*. New Haven: Community Action Institute (CPI), (2nd draft), 1965.

Kahane, Rabbi M. *Never again*. New York: Pyramid Books, 1972.

Kerner Commission (U.S. National Advisory Commission on Civil Disorders). *Report*. Washington, D.C.: U.S. Government Printing Office, 1968.

Kozol, J. *Death at an early age*. New York: Bantam Books, 1970.

Levine, M., & Levine, A. Social change and human behavior: Dependency, deviance, or diversity. Paper presented at a symposium, *The contributions of psychoanalysis to community psychology*, Adelphi University, 1968.

Liebow, E. *Tally's Corner: A study of Negro street corner man*. Boston: Little, Brown, 1967.

Lifton, R. J. Protean man. *Partisan Review*, 1968, *35*.

Mark, V. H., & Ervin, F. R. *Violence and the brain*. New York: Harper & Row, 1970.

McIntyre, D. Two schools, one psychologist. In F. Kaplan & S. B. Sarason (eds.), *The psycho-educational clinic: Collected papers and research*. Boston: State of Massachusetts Press, 1969.

McLuhan, M. & Fiore, Q. *The medium is the message*. New York: Bantam Books, 1967.

Moynihan, D. P. *The Negro family: The case for national action*. Washington, D.C.: U.S. Department of Labor, 1965.

Procumier, R. K. Letter of intent regarding neurosurgical treatment of violent inmates. In J. Agel (ed.), *Rough Times*. New York: Ballantine Books, 1973.

Sarason S. B. *The culture of the school and the problem of change.* Boston: Allyn & Bacon, 1971.

Sarason, S. B., Levine, M., Goldenberg, I. I., Cherlin, D. L. Bennett, E. M. *Psychology in community settings.* New York: John Wiley & Sons, 1966.

Seale, B. *Seize the time.* New York: Random House, 1970.

Slater, P. E. *The pursuit of loneliness: American culture at the breaking point.* Boston: Beacon Press, 1970.

Toffler, A. *Future shock.* New York: Random House, 1970.

Chapter 2

Ellison, R. *Invisible man.* New York: Modern Library, 1952.

Ryan W. *Blaming the victim.* New York: Vintage Books, 1971.

Chapter 3

Adams, P., & McDonald, N. Clinical cooling out of poor people. *American Journal of Orthopsychiatry,* 1968, *38* (4).

Agel, J. (ed.), *Rough times.* New York: Ballantine Books, 1973.

Albee, G. W. *Mental health manpower trends.* New York: Basic Books, 1959.

American Friends Service Committee. *Struggle for justice: A report on crime and punishment in America.* New York: Hill & Wang, 1971.

Aptheker, B. The social functions of the prisons in the United States. In A. Y. Davis (ed.), *If they come in the morning.* New York: Signet Books, 1971.

Buber, M. *The writings of Martin Buber.* New York: Meridian Books, 1956.

Camus, A. *The myth of Sysyphus and other essays.* New York: Vintage Books, 1959.

Chesler, P. *Women and madness.* New York: Doubleday & Co., 1973.

Clark, T., & Jaffe, D. T. *Toward a radical therapy.* New York: Gordon and Breach, 1973.

Cleaver, E. *Soul on ice.* New York: Dell Publishing Co., 1968.

Cloward, R., & Elman, R. Poverty, Injustice, and the Welfare State. *The Nation,* March 7, 1966.

Cloward, R., & Piven, F. *Regulating the poor: The function of public welfare in America.* New York: Random House, 1971.

Coles, R. Rural upheaval: Confrontation and accommodation. In J. L. Sundquist (ed.), *On fighting poverty*. New York. Basic Books, 1969.

Davis, A. Y. (ed.), *If they come in the morning*. New York: Signet Books, 1971.

de Chenne, T. In defense of individual therapy. In J. Agel (ed.), *Rough times*. New York: Ballantine Books, 1973.

Dohrenwend, B. Social status, stress, and psychological symptoms. *American Journal of Public Health*, 1967, *57* (4).

Elman, R. M. *The poorhouse state: The American way of life on public assistance*. New York: Random House, 1966.

Fuchs, E. How teachers learn to help children fail. *Transaction*, 1968, *5* (9).

Ginzburg, R. *100 Years of lynchings*. New York: Lancer Books, 1962.

Goldenberg, I. I. (ed.), *The helping professions in the world of action*. Lexington, Mass.: Heath & Co., 1973.

Goldenberg, I. I. Alternatives to incarcerating the youthful offender: The perpeuation of old myths vs. the development of a new reality. *Journal of Community Psychology*, 1973, *1* (3).

Goldenberg, I. I., Moore, M., Keating, E., Garofalo, R., Tucker, B. Cox, G., Libertoff, K., White, D., Dweck, J. *Employment and addiction: Perspectives on existing business and treatment practices* (Final Report, U.S. Department of Labor Grant No. 92-25-71-05). Cambridge, Mass.: Harvard University, 1972.

Goodman, P. The freedom to be academic. *The Cambridge Review*, 1956, *5*.

Greenlee, S. *The spook who sat by the door*. New York: Bantam Books, 1973.

Hebb, D. O. *The organization of behavior*. New York: John Wiley & Sons, 1949.

Hebb, D. O. *A textbook of psychology*. London: W. B. Saunders Co., 1958.

Katkin, E. S., & Sibley, R. F. Psychological consultation at Attica State Prison: Post-hoc reflections on some precursors to a disaster. In I. I. Goldenberg (ed.), *The helping professions in the world of action*. Lexington, Mass.: D. C. Heath & Co., 1973.

Keniston, K *The uncommitted*. New York: Harcourt, Brace and World, 1965.

Kurtis, C. *Drug abuse as a business problem*. New York: Chamber of Commerce, 1970.

Langner, T., & Michaels, S. *Life stress and mental health: The midtown Manhattan study*. New York: The Free Press, 1963.

Lerner, M. *Education and a radical humanism*. Columbus: Ohio State University Press, 1962.

Marcuse, H. *Essay on liberation*. Boston: Beacon Press, 1970.

May, R. Centrality of the problems of anxiety in our day. In M. Stein, A. J. Vidich, & D. M. White (eds.), *Identity and anxiety*. Glencoe, Ill.: The Free Press, 1960.

McArthur, A. V. *The experience of release from prison: Implications for the creation of alternative correctional programs*. Paper delivered at the annual convention of the Eastern Psychological Association, Washington, D.C., April 1973.

Paros, L. Prepping the poor. In I. I. Goldenberg (ed.), *The helping professions in the world of action*. Lexington, Mass.: D. C. Heath & Co., 1973.

Patterson, H., & Conrad, E. *Scottsboro boy*. New York: Bantam Books, 1950.

Rae-Grant, G. A., Gladwin, T., & Bower, E. M. Mental health, social competence, and the war on poverty. *American Journal of Orthopsychiatry*, 1965.

Reckless, W. C. *The crime problem*. New York: Appleton-Century-Crofts, 1950.

Regal, L. *Personal communication*. Cambridge, 1974.

Reich, C. A. *The greening of America*. New York: Random House, 1970.

Reiff, R. Mental health, manpower, and institutional change. *American Psychologist*, 1966, *21*.

Reppucci, N. D., Sarata, B. P. V., Saunders, J. T., McArthur, A. V., & Michlin, L. We bombed in Mountville: Lessons learned in consultation to a correctional facility for adolescent offenders. In I. I. Goldenberg (ed.), *The helping professions in the world of action*. Lexington, Mass.: D. C. Heath & Co., 1973.

Riesman, D., Glazer, N., & Denny, R. *The lonely crowd*. New Haven: Yale University Press, 1950.

Rosenthal, R., Jacobson, L. *Pygmalion in the classroom*. New York: Holt, Rinehart and Winston, 1968.

Sanders, M. K., & Alinsky, S. *The professional radical: Conversations with Saul Alinsky.* New York: Perennial Library, 1970.

Sarbin, T. R. *The myth of the criminal type* (Monday evening papers, no. 18). Middletown, Conn.: Center for Advanced Studies, Wesleyan University, 1969.

Sartre, J-P. *Anti-Semite and Jew.* New York: Schocken Books, 1948.

Slater, P., & Bennis, W. *The temporary society.* New York: Harper & Row, 1968.

Stein, A. Strategies of failure. *Harvard Educational Review,* 1971, *41* (2).

Stein, M. R., Vidich, A. J., & White, D. M. (eds.), *Identity and anxiety.* Glencoe, Ill.: The Free Press, 1960.

Steiner, G. *The role of psychologists in the criminal justice system: A conceptual analysis.* Paper delivered at the annual convention of the Eastern Psychological Association, Washington, D.C., April 1973.

Stewart, W. W. (ed.), *Drug abuse in industry.* Miami: Halos & Associates, 1970.

Strauss, A: Medical ghettoes. *Transaction,* May 1967.

Sutherland, E. H., & Cressey, D. R. *Principles of criminology.* New York: J. B. Lippincott Co., 1955.

Tawney, R. H. *Religion and the rise of capitalism.* New York: Harcourt, Brace & Co., 1926.

U.S. Department of Labor. *Manpower report of the president.* Washington, D.C.: U.S. Government Printing Office, 1970.

U.S. Department of Labor. *Manpower report of the president.* Washington, D.C.: U.S. Government Printing Office, 1971.

U.S. prisons: Schools for crime. *Time,* January 18, 1971.

Valentine, C. A. *Culture and poverty.* Chicago: University of Chicago: University of Chicago Press, 1968.

Wechsberg, J. (ed.), *The murderers among us.* New York: Bantam Books, 1968.

Wilkor, A., & Rasor, R. Psychiatric aspects of drug addiction. *American Journal of Medicine,* 1953, *14* (5).

Zeiger, H. A. (ed.), *The case against Adolph Eichmann.* New York: Signet Books, 1960.

Chapter 4

Alinsky, S. D. *Reveille for radicals.* New York: Vintage Books, 1969.

Alinsky, S. D. *Rules for radicals*. New York: Vintage Books, 1971.

Altshuler, A. A. Community control: *The black demand for participation in large American cities*. New York: Pegasus, 1970.

Aronowitz, S. Poverty, politics, and community organization. *Studies on the Left*, 1964, 4 (3).

Beal, R. M. Double jeopardy: To be black and female. In R. Morgan (ed.), *Sisterhood is powerful*. New York: Vintage Books, 1970.

Bing, S. R., & Breslin, T. *State of danger: Childhood lead paint poisoning in Massachusetts*. Boston: Massachusetts Advocacy Center, 1974.

Brown, S. R., Jr. *Storefront organizing*. New York: Pyramid Books, 1972.

Citizens Research and Investigation Committee, & Tackwood, L. E. *The glass house tapes*. New York: Avon Books, 1973.

Cloward, R. A., & Elman, R. M. Advocacy in the ghetto. *Transaction*, December 1966.

Coles, R. Like it is in the Alley. *Daedalus*, Fall 1968.

Dellinger, D. The future of non-violence. *Studies on the Left*, 1965, 5 (1).

Ecklein, J. L., & Lauffer, A. A. *Community organizers and social planners*. New York: John Wiley & Sons, 1972.

Edmonds, R. *Minimums and maximums: A theory and design of social service reform*. Paper presented at the Harvard University Public Policy Series, Cambridge, Mass., April 16, 1974.

Gans, H. J. The new radicalism: Sect or action movement. *Studies on the Left*, 1965, 5 (3).

Garofalo, R. L. *Entropy, Inc.: An innovative public charity*. Unpublished doctoral dissertation, Harvard University, Graduate School of Education, 1974.

Garofalo, R. L. *Neighborhood-based group homes: A training manual*. New Haven: TRI-RYC, Inc., 1974.

Goldenberg, I. I. Direct revenue-sharing with the poor: An alternative model for future programs in the area of human and institutional renewal. In R. Thompson (ed.), *Models and strategies*. Boston: TDS, 1973.

Haley, J. *The power tactics of Jesus Christ and other essays*. New York: Avon Books, 1969.

Harrington, M. *The other America*. New York: Macmillan, 1962.

Hayden, T. On the demise of ERAP. In K. Sale (ed.), *SDS*. New York: Random House, 1973.

Kelly, J. G. Ecological constraints on mental health services. *American Psychologist*, 1966, *21* (6).

Levine, M. *Some postulates of community mental health practice* (prepublication report). New Haven: Yale University, 1967.

Libertoff, K. *Runaway youth and social network interaction*. Unpublished thesis prospective, Harvard University, Graduate School of Education, 1974.

Marris, P., & Rein, M. *Dilemmas of social reform*. New York: Atherton Press, 1967.

Oppenheimer, M. *The urban guerilla*. Chicago: Quadrangle Books, 1969.

Roszak, T. *The making of a counter culture*. New York: Doubleday & Co., 1969.

Rustin, B. *Civil disobedience*. (Occasional papers). Santa Barbara, Calif.: Center for the Study of Democratic Institutions, 1966.

Sarason, S. B. *The creation of settings and the future societies*. London: Jossey-Bass, 1972.

Smith, M. B., & Hobbes, N. The community and the community mental health center. *American Psychologist*, 1966, *21* (6).

Uhlig, D. *Toward loving educational action*. Unpublished doctoral dissertation, Harvard University, Graduate School of Education, 1974.

Yolles, S. F. The role of the psychologist in comprehensive community mental health centers. *American Psychologist*, 1966, *21* (1).

Chapter 5

Argyris, C. *Organization and Innovation*. Homewood, Ill.: Richard D. Irwin, 1965.

Bradford, L. P., Gibb, J. R., & Benne, K. D. (Eds). *T-group theory and laboratory method* New York: John Wiley & Sons, 1964.

Cleaver, E. *Soul on ice*. New York: Dell Publishing Co., 1968.

Darrach, B. Gropeshrink. *Time*, July 27, 1970.

Genet, J. The members of the assembly. In H. Hayes (ed.), *Smiling through the apocalypse: Esquire's history of the sixties*. New York: The McCall Publishing Co., 1969.

Gibb, J. R. Sensitivity training as a medium for personal growth and improved interpersonal relations. *Interpersonal Development*, 1970, *1* (1).

Goldenberg, I. I. *America: Our recent past and contemporary lifestyles.* Address delivered at the commencement ceremonies of Eastern Connecticut State College, Willimantic, Conn., May 28, 1972.

Hayes, H. (ed.), *Smiling through the Apocalypse: Esquire's history of the sixties.* New York: The McCall Publishing Co., 1969.

Holmes, J. C. The philosophy of the beat generation. In S. Krim (ed.), *The beats.* Greenwich, Conn.: Fawcett Publications, 1960.

Howard, J. *Please touch.* New York: Dell Publishing Co., 1970.

Lakin, M. Some ethical issues in sensitivity training. *American Psychologist,* 1969, *24* (10).

Lester, J. *Look out, whitey! Black power's gon' get your mama.* New York: The Dial Press, 1968.

Lieberman, M., Yalom, I., & Miles, M. Encounter: The leader makes the difference. *Psychology Today,* March 1973.

McReynolds, D. The choice: 1776 or 1984. In D. Rader (ed.), *Defiance #3: A radical review.* New York: Paperback Library, 1971.

Magic Animal Farm in Communities: A Journal of Cooperative Living, 1974 (8).

Maliver, B. L. Encounter groupers up against the wall, *New York Times Magazine,* January 3, 1971.

Marcuse, H. Charles Reich—a negative view. *New York Times,* November 6, 1970.

Nobile, P. (ed.), *The con III controversy: The critics look at the greening of America.* New York: Pocket Books, 1971.

Packard, V. *The status seekers.* New York: David McKay Co., 1959.

Perls, F. S. *Gestalt therapy verbatim.* New York: Bantam Books, 1971.

Reich, C. A. *The greening of America.* New York: Random House, 1970.

Riesman, D., Glazer, N., & Denny, R. *The lonely crowd.* New Haven: Yale University Press, 1950.

Schlesinger, A. M., Jr. *A thousand days: John F. Kennedy in the White House.* Boston: Houghton Mifflin Co., 1965.

Schutz, W. Joy: *Expanding human awareness.* New York: Grove Press, 1967.

Singer, D. L., Whiton, M. B., & Fried, M. L. An alternative to traditional mental health and consultation in schools: A social systems and group process approach. *Journal of School Psychology* 1970, *8.*

von Hoffman, N. The soft revolution. *Washington Post*, 1970.

Ways, M. The real greening of America. *Fortune*, November 1970.

Whyte, W. H., Jr. *The organization man.* New York: David McKay Co., 1959.

Winthrop, H. Abuses of sensitivity training on the American Campus. *Bulletin of the Menniger Clinic*, 1971, *35* (1).

Chapter 6

Alinsky, S. D. *Rules for radicals.* New York: Vintage Books, 1971.

Bugental, J. F. T. (ed.), *Challenges of humanistic psychology.* New York: McGraw-Hill, 1967.

Glazer, N., & Moynihan, D. P. *Beyond the melting pot.* Cambridge: The M.I.T. Press, 1963.

Goldenberg, I. I. The clinician and the community: Contemporary responsibilities and historical imperatives. *Annals of the New York Academy of Sciences*, 1969, *31* (6).

Goldenberg, I. I. The relationship of the university to the community: Implications for community mental health programs. In H. E. Mitchell (ed.), *The university and the urban crisis.* Community Psychology Series, II, 1974.

Harvard University, *The nature and purposes of the university.* J. T. Dunlop, (chairman), A discussion memorandum, interim report. Cambridge, Mass., January 1971.

Maslow, A. H. *Motivation and personality.* New York: Harper, 1954.

Polanyi, M. *Personal knowledge.* New York: Harper, 1962.

Schlesinger, A. M., Jr. *A thousand days: John F. Kennedy in the White House.* Boston: Houghton-Mifflin Co., 1965.

Skinner, B. F. *Beyond freedom and dignity.* New York: Bantam Books, 1971.

Walters, R. H. Mechanomorphism: A new term for an old mode of thought, *Psychological Review*, 1948, *55.*

INDEX